AUNTIE
RITA

AUNTIE
RITA

Rita Huggins and Jackie Huggins

Sadly Rita passed away peacefully on
27 August 1996 surrounded by her family

Aboriginal Studies Press
Canberra

First published in 1994 by
Aboriginal Studies Press
for the Australian Institute of Aboriginal Studies
GPO Box 553 Canberra ACT 2601.

Reprinted 1996, 2005, 2010

The views expressed in this publication are those of the author and
not necessarily those of the Australian Institute of Aboriginal and
Torres Strait Islander Studies.

National Library of Australia Cataloguing in Publication Data:

Huggins, Rita
Auntie Rita

ISBN 0 85575 248 3

1. Huggins, Rita [2.] Aborigines, Australian — Biography.
I. Huggins, Jackie. II. Title

994 0049915

Edited by Alison Ravenscroft
Produced by Aboriginal Studies Press
Typeset in Palacio 11/13
Printed in Australia by Pirion Pty Limited

Cover image by Leah King-Smith, from photographs by
Angela Bailey and Jane Jacobs

This book is dedicated to
Albert and Rose,
Jack,
Gloria and Kenny

Contents

Holt

Rosie Holt was the daughter of Lucy a full-blood Pitjara woman from the Maranoa, and a white man by the name of Keswick who in Tindale's research was known as Keswick.

She had four other brothers and sisters. Lucy was married to Conway of Woorabinda.

Albert Holt was the son of Maggie, a full-blood woman from Springsure, and a white station owner who owned the Wulurdargle Station south of Springsure. Maggie married a Bundle from Springsure, however had children to two whitemen. Albert was one of them.

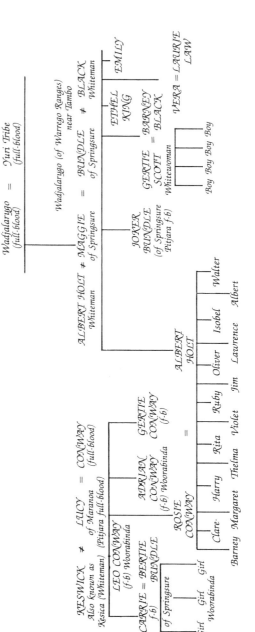

Holt-Conway family tree, as recorded by anthropologist Norman Tindale, 5 November 1938, Cherbourg

Foreword

Rita Huggins is one of those universal spirits who makes indelible footprints on the hearts of those who have ever met her.

Generous of spirit, she has enriched people by her presence.

After meeting Rita Huggins, one could never ask, 'Rita who?' Bland and insipid are words that could never be applied to her.

For those who have never met her, you can now read her story.

It is not a fashionable story of how she suddenly found her 'Aboriginal identity'. On the contrary, it is a story of an Aboriginal woman who, because she was 'cosmetically apparent', had to endure the hurts and innuendoes of racism which was and has been the lot of fellow visible Aboriginal people in Australia.

Her reactions to those hurts and innuendoes of racism meant that, in turn, Rita Huggins was sometimes passionate, fiery, fiesty, quiet, dignified, reflective, but never bitter and unforgiving.

How she managed to retain her warrior spirit, along with a lack of bitterness, has both inspired and intrigued younger Aboriginal women of my generation.

My life has been enriched through knowing her and her trials and triumphs.

FOREWORD

This vivacious and dynamic woman — in all her hues and all her multitude of emotions — is proof of the enduring spirit of Aboriginal people in this country, particularly Aboriginal women.

Rita Huggins's story is first and foremost about being Aboriginal in Australia, being a woman, and last but not least, being a truly universal spirit.

Lillian Holt

Lillian Holt

x

Writing the Book

I HAVE OFTEN WONDERED why we like to read books about the lives of other people. Perhaps we are interested in what shapes people, or maybe we're just plain busy-bodies.

This book tells the story of my life. These are my own recollections. I speak only for myself and not how others would expect me to speak. The book exposes me and my family. But I can only be myself and hope people can judge me on that, whether it be good or bad. I'm not perfect, just Auntie Rita.

We want the book to be a record for my children and their children and other members of my family. Hopefully it will speak to other people, too, including those white people who want to know what the story looks like from the Aboriginal side.

This book was such a huge task. We didn't realise when we began how enormous it would be. Far from sitting down and writing when a thought came to mind, it has to follow some order. But we found it can't always do that so smoothly. People's lives aren't like that. Lives jump here, there and everywhere and then return to the beginning and start again. Like an Aboriginal meeting, as you'll know if you've been to one.

It's like time in Aboriginal society. In the old days there wasn't time like we think of it now, and there are still ways today when time isn't important to us as it is to migaloos. I've noticed it in places where our people can still live their old ways like Ti Tree and Alice Springs. The old people sit for hours. You can't say, 'I'll meet you at seven o'clock' and expect someone to show up just because your watch is on seven. With Murrie time, it can be hours later and no one bats an eyelid. In the old days the sun and moon told us the time.

Family and health crises arose during the writing of this book. Since doing this book I have lost another brother and two sisters, a nephew and some dear friends. Interruptions came as family members came to me with their problems. A year ago I had a serious illness but was determined to see my book published.

The title of this book comes from the term 'Auntie' that we use in our communities. It is one of respect and affection. You don't have to be blood relations or anything. Everyone calls me Auntie or Nan.

There are some parts of my life that I probably didn't want to have in the book because to me they are shame jobs. But they are part of the story and Jackie tells me, in her loving way, that I don't need to feel ashamed. Look who's talking! My story is not rare among Aboriginal women.

There are, though, other things that I just cannot speak about because they are too painful to remember. These things I must keep to myself. Much has been done to me and my people that we find hard to talk about. One of the things that amazes people is that we have managed to survive without a huge amount of outward bitterness. Aboriginal people of all generations, and for very good reasons, withhold their bitterness about the injustices that have happened and still continue to happen today. I'm not sure why I let go of my bitterness. I certainly remember those feelings but try to replace them with more positive feelings. That is how I have survived, and remain feeling strong.

Rita Huggins

*T*his *book is the result of my mother's and my combined efforts and of our mutual Aboriginality. It is born out of so many years of our talking. During the book's writing, we have had many arguments (fighting with our tongues, as Rita calls it) and some of this has not been resolved, continues and remains evident in these pages. In our talking are reflected both the things we have in common and the differences that arise between two Aboriginal women a generation apart; one born in 1921 and raised on a mission, the other born 'free' in the '50s. Our differences reflect changed political groundings. For instance, for Rita, 'Black' is only used among ourselves and with those non-Aboriginal people we trust, because to use it publicly raises negative connotations and prejudice, whereas for my generation Black has been reclaimed with pride.*

In the text are some words and expressions that will be unfamiliar to most non-Aboriginal readers. There are Pitjara, Wakka Wakka and Aboriginal English ways of talking. We made a decision not to differentiate these words in the text because they are part of our natural way of speech. This may cause some unsettling and confusing moments for a white reader. However, there is a glossary for those unfamiliar with our languages.

After getting many of Rita's memories on tape, I began, through naivity, to translate my mother's voice, trying to do it justice while knowing that this book would have a predominantly white audience. This was my first cardinal sin. (The second was losing the disk!) Although Rita speaks a standard English, her voice often got lost amid my own as I attempted to 'protect' her from non-Aboriginal critics. Black writers grapple with this all the time. But Aboriginal ways of speaking need to be maintained and protected, for they are authentic, precious and irreplaceable.

The separation of voices here will I hope prove to be one of the book's strengths. Now I am not speaking for my mother but to her, with her, and about her.

All this could not have come about without good editorial skills. I had been cynical of white editorial intervention, but with Alison

3

Ravenscroft we entered into a productive collaboration. The editing was unimposing and enabling, and there soon developed a trust between Rita, Alison and I. Our relationship has been a crucial factor in a mutually satisfying outcome.

But the history of writing this book has not always been a happy one. I am very grateful for the financial support I received from AIATSIS to write the book in the first place. However, difficulties arose that are common problems for Black writers. We still face the fact that most publishing in this country is controlled by white people who have very little knowledge of our culture. White publishers need to develop more co-operative relations with Black writers, finding ways of involving Black people more closely with production decisions.

The writing of this book was an attempt to reclaim the history of our people. To do this is to encounter a double fold of silence. Each fold is of the same cloth — two centuries of colonisation. There are the acts of violence that attempted to alienate (with varying degrees of success). Black people's access to knowledge of their own culture and its history: taking people from their lands, separating children from their parents, insisting on the surrender of traditional languages and customs and the adoption of European ways. This list goes on, and continues into the present. There is another order of silence again, though, and this is the silence that you meet in Aboriginal elders who cannot bear to speak of the humiliations and mutilations they have experienced and which they have witnessed.

One of the many contemporary forms that the silencing takes is the resistance that Aboriginal people meet in white bureaucrats when they attempt to see Aboriginal records. Files were compiled on every person who had lived on a reserve, in Queensland and elsewhere, and often were continued long after the person had moved on. As part of writing this book, we sought access to my mother's personal files held by the Department of Family Services and Aboriginal and Islander Affairs in 1990. When I first made enquiries about seeing my mother's file, I was made to watch across a huge desk as two white public servants turned the pages. Watch, not touch. The men stopped at various pages and read

4

them, and made comments to each other that I couldn't hear. These gatekeepers behaved as if the files were their personal property whereas they are in fact part of my people's inheritance, part of a history that remains to be recovered and claimed.

A white friend of ours had far greater access to these files than we would ever have. He was taken to be a credentialled researcher whereas I am dismissed as just another Blackfella wanting to know some family roots.

Finally, with the assistance of a newly appointed Aboriginal member of staff, we saw the file. We had been forewarned that the file could contain hurtful material and to remember the times in which it was written and the paternalistic nature of those who wrote it. Little has changed. Nothing could really have prepared my mother for the experience of reading her files. The first entry is 1942 and the last 1974 — thirty-two years of surveillance. Whether my mother's activism around Aboriginal issues prolonged this policing is hard to tell, but it is commonly known that most, if not all, ex-inmates of reserves had files kept on them regardless of whether they were politically active. The file told of bills outstanding from Myers in 1968, a thirty dollar rent bill. It told of the time my mother ran away from the mission. As Rita tells it:

It told all the bad things in my life and none of the positive, of which there were many. Anyone would think I was a murderer. But I guess there has to be something to keep those dorry public servants in a job. There were even comments in the files on the lives of my children who were born free, not on the mission.

Assimilationist policies of successive state and federal governments over several decades explicitly articulated the racism in this country and the rejection of Aboriginal values. However, these moves towards cultural genocide failed and instead Aboriginals have become successively more visible and vocal in the face of attempted annihilation, and a great store of historical and cultural knowledge has begun to surface. Oral histories, storytellings, philosophy, biography and autobiography are coming to be published. I feel humble to be a recipient of this knowledge. Recording and publishing the memories of elderly Aboriginals is an especially urgent

5

task, *otherwise important aspects of Australian history that our elders can pass on will be lost forever.*

My mother is a fine storyteller. I remember most of her stories, probably much better than she realises. She recalls for her audience all the details of the past with the vividness of the present. To work with her in seeing these stories published has been a labour of love and in some way might compensate her for the many sacrifices she has made and acknowledge the love, strength, wisdom and inspiration she has given to me and so many others. Aboriginal women are not so well known outside their communities. The media gives their work scant attention. But among their own people, many women are known for their great contributions, and respected and appreciated for it. I am proud to say that my mother is one such person.

Jackie Huggins

CHAPTER ONE

Don't Cry, Gunduburries

I WAS ONLY A SMALL CHILD when we were taken from my born country. I only remember a little of those times there but my memories are very precious to me. Most of my life has been spent away from my country but before I tell you any more of my story I want to tell you what I remember about the land I come from. It will always be home, the place I belong to.

My born country is the land of the Bidjara–Pitjara people, and is known now as Carnarvon Gorge, 600 kilometres northwest of Brisbane. This was also the land of the Kairi, Nuri, Karingbal, Longabulla, Jiman and Wadja people. Our people lived in this land since time began. In our land are waterfalls, waterholes and creeks where we swam and where the older people fished. Our mob always seemed cool, even on the hottest days, because the country was like an oasis. There were huge king ferns. I believe they have been described as living fossils because their form has not changed for thousands of years.

We were never left with empty bellies. The men hunted kangaroos, goannas, lizards, snakes and porcupines with spears and boomerangs. The women gathered berries, grubs, wild plums, honey and waterlilies, and yams and other roots with their digging sticks. Children stayed with the women when the men hunted so that they wouldn't be close to the hunt and frighten

7

away the animals. The creeks gave us lots of food, too — yellow belly and jew, perch and eel.

My mother would use leaves from trees to make soap for washing our bodies with, and unfortunately for us kids there was no excuse not to take a bogey. I remember goanna fat being used for cuts and scratches as well as being a soothing ointment for aches and pains. Eucalyptus leaves were used for coughs, and the bark of certain trees for rashes and open wounds. Witchetty grubs helped babies' teething, and we used charcoal for cleaning teeth.

There were huge cliffs and rocks, riddled with caves where many of my people's paintings were. Most caves and rock faces showed my people's stencilled hands, weapons and tools, and there were engravings here, too. Fertility symbols and the giant serpent tell us of the spiritual significance of the place. This place is old. My people and their art were here long before the whiteman came.

The caves were cool places in summer and warm places in winter, and offered shelter when the days were windy or when there was rain. They offered a safe place for the women bringing new life into the world. As had happened for my mother and her mother before her, going back generation after generation, I was born in the sanctuary of one of those caves. My mother would tell us how my grandmother would wash my mother's newborn babies in the nearby creek, place them in a cooliman and carry them back to suckle on my exhausted mother's breast.

We lived in humpies, or gunyahs, that the men built from tree branches, bark and leaves. Gum resin held them together. We would sleep inside the gunyahs, us children arguing for the warm place closest to Mama, a place usually kept for the youngest children. More gunyahs would be built as they were needed in this serene valley that had nurtured my people since time began.

My mother, Rose, had a Bidjara–Pitjara mother known as Lucy Conway from the Maranoa River and a white father who was never married to her mother. I never knew who her father was. I don't know much about the contact my mother had with whites. She had a whiteman's name, but she also had a tribal name, Gylma, and she spoke language and knew the old ways. My father, Albert Holt, was the son of a Yuri woman known as Maggie Bundle and a whiteman, the owner of Wealwandangie Station. My father was named after that man. My grandmother may have been working at the homestead. Dadda was brought up on the station, away from his mother's people. When he grew older he wanted to be with Aboriginal people, and started visiting the camps. He saw my mother there and wanted to marry her. After that, he stayed in the camp with her, and then the children started coming.

One winter's night, troopers came riding on horseback through our camp. My father went to see what was happening, and my mother stayed with her children to try to stop us from being so frightened. One trooper I remember clearly. Perhaps he was sorry for what he was doing, because he gave me some fruit — a banana, something as unknown to me as the whiteman who offered it. My mother saw, and cried out to me, 'Barjun! Barjun!'.

Dadda and some of the older men were shouting angrily at the officials. We were being taken away from our lands. We didn't know why, nor imagined what place we would be taken to. I saw the distressed look on my parents' faces and knew something was terribly wrong. We never had time to gather up any belongings. Our camp was turned into a scattered mess — the fire embers still burning.

What was to appear next out of the bush took us all by surprise and we nearly turned white with fright. It was a huge cage with four round things on it which, when moved by the man in the cabin in front, made a deafening sound, shifting the ground and flattening the grass, stones and twigs beneath it. We had never seen a cattle truck before. A strong smell surrounded us as we entered the truck and we saw brown stains on the wooden floor.

9

They packed us in like cattle with hardly any room to move. The troopers threw a few blankets over us (we thought they were strange animal skins). There weren't enough blankets for all of us, and so the older people gave them to us younger ones while they went without. The night was cold and colder still on the back of the open truck.

It took the whole night across rough dirt tracks to reach our first destination of Woorabinda Aboriginal Settlement. Woori was a dry and dusty place compared to the home we were forced to leave. My memory of the place at that time is not clear but I do remember seeing some gunyahs and some people there watching us. The people were not smiling — just like us. Although curious to see us, the people did not come too far outside their gunyahs but watched from a safe distance as our older people were unloaded by the troopers.

I will never forget how they huddled, frightened, cold and crying in their blankets. Some of our old relations were wrenched from our arms and lives that day and it is for them that I shed my tears. One old lady broke away from the others and screamed, 'Don't take my gunduburries! Don't take my gunduburries!' as the truck moved off, taking us away from her. After running a small distance she was stopped and held by the officials who wanted to keep 'wild bush Blacks' on these reserves.

My father's ashen face told the story and we were never to see our old people again. Dadda could never bring himself to speak about it. Our tribe was torn away — finished. Perhaps the hurt and pain always remained for him. It was understandable then why he would hate and rebel against the authorities for the rest of his days after what they did to our people.

The old people from both Cherbourg and Woorabinda always told the story that the 'full bloods' were sent to Woorabinda and the fairer-skinned to Cherbourg. Both my parents were considered 'half-castes' because they both had white fathers. I had always wondered why our people were split up and found out sometime in my twenties that the government people thought that those of us who looked whiter would more easily assimilate than the darker ones, but this was not so. Sometimes it was vice versa. But skin never mattered to us. It was how we felt about being Aboriginal that counted. It was when I was in my twenties, too, that I was given a certificate which specified my 'breed'. 'Cross out description not required', it said. 'Full blood, half caste, quadroon.'

The truck went on, travelling for two terrible days, going further south. As if in a funeral procession, we were loud in our silence. We were all in mourning. I can't remember what we had to eat or drink, or where we stopped on the journey, but by the time we reached our destination we were numb with cold, tiredness and hunger. And this new country was so different from our country — flat, no hills and valleys, arid and cleared of trees.

Camp at Cherbourg (people and date unknown)

11

It was Barambah Reserve (renamed Cherbourg in 1932) that we'd been brought to, just outside Murgon on the Barambah River. Here we were separated from each other into rough houses — buildings that seemed so strange to me then, with their walls so straight. Each family was fenced off from the others into their own two little rooms where you ate and slept. The houses were little cells, all next to each other in rows. A prison. No wonder that, along with 'mission', 'reserve', 'settlement', 'Muddy Flats' and 'Guna Valley', Cherbourg has been named 'prison' and 'concentration camp' by Aboriginal people. The place in fact had its own gaol. A prison in a prison. There were white and Aboriginal areas. Government authorities and teachers stayed away from us, and their areas were off-limits to all Aboriginal people.

One of the Aboriginal living areas was called top camp, and it was dotted with gunyahs. It was here that Annie Evans lived with her large family. She was the first person to greet us when we arrived, and gave us food. Her generosity was never forgotten by my parents or by myself. Her daughter Barbara was my age and we became best friends and stayed that way all our lives.

No one had the right to remove us from our traditional lands and to do what they did to us. We were once the proud custodians of our land and now our way of life became controlled by insensitive people who knew nothing about us but thought they knew everything. They even chose how and where we could live. We had to stay in one place now while the whiteman could roam free.

We took a trip back to my born country in 1986. It was the first time I had been back since that night we were taken over sixty years before. Tourism has taken its toll in the area, but the place still has its wild beauty. I felt the call of my people billowing through the trees and welcoming me home again. I saw the smiling faces of my elders, the ambers of the campfire, heard the women singing. In my heart was such a deep happiness because I knew I was home again. 'Rita Huggins was born somewhere out there', I said over and over again in my mind.

*R*eturning to my mother's born country as she refers to it complemented my own sense of identity and belonging, and my pride in this. It was important that together we make this trip as she had been insisting for quite some time, pining for her homelands. We shared a special furthering of our mother–daughter bond during this time, although we argued incessantly about nothing as usual or, as she calls it, 'fighting with our tongues'. I began to gain an insight into and understanding of her obvious attachment and relationship to her country and how our people had cared for this place way before the Royal Geographic Society and park rangers ever clapped eyes on it. The way my mother moved around, kissed the earth and said her prayers will have a lasting effect on my soul and memory because she was paying homage and respect to her ancestors who had passed on long ago but whose presence we could both intensely feel.

The land of my mother and my maternal grandmother is my land, too. It will be passed down to my children and successive generations, spiritually, in the manner that has been carried on for thousands of years. Fate dictates that nothing will ever change this. As Rita's daughter, I not only share the celebration and the pain of her experience but also the land from which we were created.

Like most Aboriginal people, it is my deeply held belief that we came from this land, hence the term 'the land is my mother'. The land is our birthing place, our cradle; it offers us connection with the creatures, the trees, the mountains and the rivers, and all living things. There are no stories of migration in our dreamtime stories. Our creation stories link us intrinsically to the earth. We are born of the earth and when we die our body and spirit go back there. This is why land is so important to us, no matter where and when we were born.

The removal of Aboriginal people from their lands has gone on since the arrival of the whiteman, and it still goes on. Alienation from *traditional lands has just taken different forms at different times. Reserves like Cherbourg and Woorabinda onto which my mother's people were placed were set up under the* Queensland Aborigines Protection and Restriction of the Sale of Opium Act *of 1897. The decades that followed the introduction of the Act were a period of acute isolation and control of Aboriginal people. Aboriginals were deliberately and systematically cut off from their traditional ways of life and made to conform to, and become dependent on, European ways. The reserves refused Aboriginals the rights to their own languages, ceremonies, religious beliefs and marriage laws, and in their place was put a culture of control and surveillance. Every action and association was monitored; employment — including any wages — was managed by the reserves' superintendents; personal relations were intervened in. Punishment, including days and nights in the gaol, sometimes in solitary confinement, was meted out with imperialist assurance.*

Reserves were supposedly established for the care and protection of Aboriginal people, and there is a double irony in that. Not only were Aboriginals subjected to humiliating treatment in the reserves, but if they needed protection it was from whites. In the decades preceding the introduction of the Act, bloody massacres had taken place in Carnarvon Gorge, and all across the country. The massacres were ritualised violence, intended to demonstrate white superiority and power. The poisoning of flour and waterholes may be common knowledge; burying Blackfellas alive in sand, tying them to trees for use in shooting practice, is less so. Who were the barbarians?

The history of violence on the frontier has only been partially addressed. More orthodox historians have tended to downplay the extent of the violences committed against Aboriginal people, and revisionist historians, such as Ray Evans and Gordon Reid, who have attempted to reconstruct the massacres around my family's area, are marginalised.

In 1857, the Jiman of the Carnarvon Gorge area, reacting against the rape of Jiman women, the dispossession of hunting grounds, and the destruction of sacred sites, killed the whites present at the Fraser homestead at the Hornet Bank Station. In revenge, whites conducted the six-month 'little war' over a vast area unrelated to the Gorge, shooting down men, women and children as they ran. No measures were taken to stop this slaughter.

The killings went on long after, and all over Australia. Aboriginal people were nearly wiped out and it is a wonder that we are alive to tell the story. Because our beginnings as Black and white Australians were steeped in bloodshed and murder, and Black survival depended on such flimsy pieces of fate, it makes it almost impossible for us to pick up the pieces, forget about it and make up.

A man of my tribe, Grandfather Chooky, witnessed the killing of sixteen white people at Cullinlaringo near Springsure in 1861. The Wills family died in this pay-back killing. The same thing had been happening there as in other places. White men stole and raped our women. This made Aboriginal people very angry and unhappy.

Grandfather Chooky is said to be an ancestor of mine, and to have been well over a hundred when he died. The whiteman believed he was a leader of our people, so he gave him a breastplate and called him King Chooky. But there weren't any kings in our culture, only elders.

'Chooky, King of Rainworth'

15

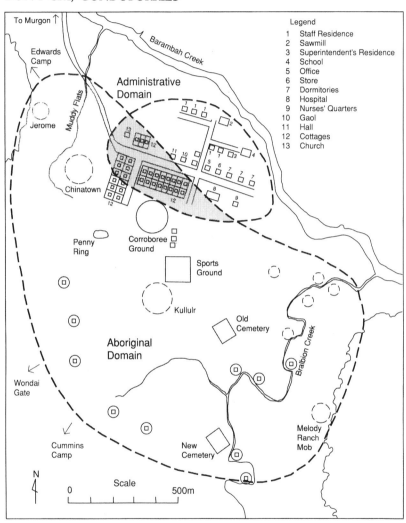

Barambah (Cherbourg) Aboriginal Settlement, 1930s (with thanks to Thom Blake)

16

Growing Up Cherbourg

M Y PEOPLE WERE MADE TO USE English words at Cherbourg rather than our Pitjara language. If we used our own language in front of the authorities we would face punishment and be corrected in the Queen's English. The authorities tried to take away all our tribal ways and to replace them with English ones.

This is the way it was with our tribal names. My parents Albert and Rose were given English names by their white station owners. In turn my parents called their children: Barney, Clare, Margaret, Harry, Thelma, Rita, Violet, Jim, Ruby, Oliver, Lawrence, Isobel, Albert and Walter. It is known that at least the three eldest had tribal names as well as English ones, but we don't know anymore what they were. I don't remember whether I was ever given a tribal name. If I did, it was taken away from me when we were taken to Cherbourg.

My mother was such a fine woman. She was a big woman, although she dwindled away to a shadow before she died in 1972. She never had an argument with my father, at least not in our presence. Her work around the house was spotless. She would sweep the timber floors and then scald them with hot water and caustic soda once a week. Mama would even sweep the bare ground outside. It was as though she was in control of everything, her domain and her huge family. Our people went down to the store for rations and things for cleaning, like brooms, buckets, scrubbing brushes. They would get instructions and lessons how to use them at the store by the white officials. Mama would hide these new 'toys' up high in the trees where the kids couldn't get them. When Dadda came in from working, Mama would provide a dish, soap and towel for him before he sat down to have his meals. It was as if hygiene was a safeguard to this strange, new world we had just entered.

It must have been terrible for my mother and the others. Mama just had to do things. She had no choice. I think in her mind she must have said, 'My country, my culture, what I can do in the bush, have gone forever'. I believe she resisted a lot and never did all what the white people told her. She was never a believer of whiteman's medicine, saying it was barjun. She was a wonderful woman who evenly distributed her amazing love between all her fourteen children. The love we received from her was different from Dadda's. Although we loved and respected them both, there was a special warmth about Mama which was always there. She had a beautiful aura about her which went with her strength.

When my mother and the other women went to the hospital to have babies there was a lovely Matron Wren who always loved the Aboriginal people. But when my mother went there the first time to have Jimmy, her first baby born at Cherbourg, she felt funny about a white person touching her and a white person being the first person to touch her baby. She was so used to my grannie and my aunties and the other women in the bush delivering the babies. It really frightened her going into four walls and seeing all the instruments, a white matron and a nurse. I could imagine how she felt. It frightened her also when Matron Wren said, 'Let the baby come out', and when she did she'd look up to the heavens and think of her old mother and say, 'All finished...all gone...a new gunduburrie born now'.

We'd all rush her when she brought the new baby home. She had no napkins but we'd go to the rubbish dump looking for materials and clothes and take a knife to get the pretty buttons. Mama loved sewing, which the missionaries had taught her. The tip was in Murgon where the rich folk would throw out good things. We were too frightened to go to Murgon, frightened of the white men. Dadda would say, 'You go any further, they shoot you'. Mama would be holding the baby, looking around at where us kids would be while another held tightly onto her skirt. All the people in Cherbourg would say, 'There goes Rosie and her ducklings'. My younger brother, Wal, would come home after school and throw Mama's top up to suckle on her breast. He was about eight and it was as if she knew he was her last child. We still laugh about our baby brother today.

The government owned a store on the reserve where an official would ration out food, clothing and blankets every fortnight, but the food was only enough to last a few days. Mama usually went down with a sugarbag to collect what she could. She'd make whatever there was go around for the ever-hungry mouths. Among the rations was a lot of anything bad for health like sugar, salt, flour, tea, offal (including the inners of bullocks which we called running guts) and bibles and very little of any nutritional value. So Dadda and the boys would go hunting. They would hunt in the traditional way with spears, boomerangs and sharp sticks. In the early days, guns were not allowed to be owned by the Aboriginals on the reserves. Only the officials and the Black trackers carried them. A hunt would not pass unless several kangaroos, emus, goannas, possums, rabbits or our favourite — porcupines and carpet snakes (which still make my mouth water) — were found. Compared to the tasteless, stale meat we received in our rations, our bush tucker was always greatly appreciated.

Rose Holt,
Cherbourg,
1938

Although we had a wood stove, for many years Mama preferred to continue to cook outside.

Later, my sister Violet worked at a Murgon grocer and we would get scraps. The scraps were like Christmas to us, different sorts of things we'd never eaten before like fruit mince tarts and icing. Dinner was always on the table for Dadda when he came home. We boasted the best garden in Cherbourg at the time. There were lots of fruit trees in our yard. These were lemons, oranges, figs and mangoes.

Mama was very protective. She always kept an eye on us and knew where we were. She knew too well of the 'half-caste' kids who were taken away from their parents and her over-protectiveness as we saw it then was justified. The Aboriginal grapevine operated as much in those days as it does today. Except today its faster with things like telephones. Word of mouth passed around the coming of the white people — how far away they were, the strange animals they owned and the terrible things they did to our people like shooting, poisoning and, the worst crime, taking our children from us.

Albert Holt,
Cherbourg,
1938

She knew the value of money even though she hardly got any. She treasured it in a handkerchief which she would carry around with her. 'Spin it around' was her favourite saying and she would be careful with it to the last penny.

When letters were received from any of her children working away, she'd be overjoyed and get one of us to read it to her. Then we'd have to write back with all the news of home. How contented she'd feel that she could speak with her children when they were so far away. Her love was all consuming.

My father Albert was a proud man who lost a leg in a riding accident at work on one of the stations. He could still ride a yarraman as good as any able-bodied person. He had a particular fondness for his pipe, and for European swear words, particularly the f. word. While my father was a hard worker and good provider for all his family he never took on a whitefella's job. He never understood how migaloos work to a set time. The white way of working was so alien to our culture. Dadda was frustrated by the western way of doing things and in fact rebelled against employment forced onto other inmates. He never had and wasn't

21

about to bow down to any whiteman. In a sense I suspect he was excused by the officials because of his disability.

Dadda would regularly play cards, which again were European inventions but which he liked. Cards had been introduced to the reserve lifestyle before we arrived in Cherbourg. Gambling schools were secretly set up throughout the settlement and the habit continues to thrive today. He would spend days at such events and then return home with family peace offerings of abundant bush tucker, including our favourite wild honey which was like lollies to us. In fact, every time the food supply was short he would disappear for days, and bring back more tasty food.

He set the highest standards for us and was intolerant if we did not meet them. Lessons like honesty, reliability, respect and loyalty. The value of his standards of life, humanity and pride, were realised by his children later in our lives. Immoral conduct like chasing another person's spouse was an unforgivable crime to Dadda but perhaps the wish he wanted most for all his children was for them to marry another Aboriginal person. Absolutely not a white. His dream came almost entirely true.

He was the toughest disciplinarian you could ever meet. Unlike my mother who was even-tempered, Dadda had a volatile temper which would erupt into full-scale fury and war when stirred. We were ingrained with a sense of honesty, good manners, morals and responsibilities and if we erred we would face the consequences from Dadda. His word was law and we dared not speak back or challenge him. It was unheard of and anyway not worth the punishment he would have dished out. He owned a stockwhip and some belts which hitched up his loosely fitting trousers. These would become almost lethal weapons when he singled out one or several of us for a hiding. There was nothing on earth like his floggings. I still shudder to this day when I think of them. I got one for stealing peaches one day from Nellie McIvor's trees.

Lucy, Patty McIvor and Nellie lived next door to us. I was about nine then, and was playing in our backyard with my good mate Barbara Evans. We suddenly felt hungry and both looked over the fence at the same time to the McIvor's fat, ripe peaches on the tree. Now, we knew that this succulent fruit was heaven because Nellie often brought Mama over a huge basketful. Mm...I had indeed tasted their juicy flesh on a number of occasions before.

Without hesitation, I jumped the fence and began picking the heavily laden tree. In no time I managed to throw several peaches back over the fence to Barbara who immediately bit into them. Unfortunately in my haste and hunger I forgot about the McIvor's barking and ferocious dog Dodger who then chased me up the tree. Auntie Lucy came racing out to see what all the noise was about only to find me dangling from a branch with Dodger in hot pursuit. 'Gotcha!', she growled. 'And you can stay up there until Dadda comes home'.

By this time my best mate and loyal friend Barbara had disappeared from the face of the earth. I got gooly up with her at that and didn't speak to her for ages afterwards. I was left whimpering in the tree for about fifteen minutes before I heard a man's footsteps, followed by the distinct sound of my father's voice which grew louder and closer. Auntie Lucy must have told him. 'Knock off, Rita, you come down from that f'n tree, you thieving so-and-so!', he yelled. All the other curious kids who'd been hanging around scattered in a dozen directions.

I hung my head in shame. Dadda grabbed my arm tightly and took me home where he shoved me in a room and reached for his stockwhip. The belting began. My tears poured over my cheeks as I closed my eyes. I had never experienced pain like that before. My mother never interfered when my father disciplined any of us. When the belting was over, Mum bathed my wounds with salt water after which she wrapped them in calico. This was only to prove band-aid treatment as the wounds were much more serious and I was later hospitalised overnight.

After that, I never took a hiding for granted — or stole Nellie's peaches again. Dadda felt a lot of remorse over that incident, bringing me fruit home daily for the next month. He spoilt me totally, gave me horserides and hugs. I could tell he was deeply sorry for what he had done by the look on his face every time he saw me. Of course, I still got scolded throughout my growing-up years like my other brothers and sisters, but never again would it be as severe as that belting. Dadda mostly didn't show much affection, being the serious and stern man that he was, but we loved him deeply just the same.

Dadda would listen to the radio for hours. He had a passion for the news and political stories. During the war he would leave it on one station only. We were never game to move the dial for fear of a belting. We never heard any music or other programmes.

Dadda was a smart man, a bush lawyer by anyone's standards. He fought against the injustices of Aboriginal people on Cherbourg. He was called a stirrer by white officials because of his outspoken views and his arguments for better conditions. In fact, one Department of Native Affairs removals paper cites his occupation as 'black stirrer'.[1] Many people in his community trusted his ability to deal with the authorities. Unfortunately, he was a lone voice, and had no strong support from other residents. Many Aboriginal people in those days were too afraid of white people and the system to stand up for themselves. Much of Dadda's anger he had to keep to himself. He was such an angry man and I realise now why this was so.

Aboriginal people at that time were so quashed in their attempts to speak out. My father was a great man who attempted to speak out but was ignored and put down for his efforts. He may have been as important to the struggle in his day as Charlie Perkins has been in his, but was never ever recognised for this. If it had been recognition he'd wanted, he lived in the wrong era.

He had a regal presence about him. A 'man of high degree', although not in the clever man or medicine man mould but a man who stood out from others, a man of great intelligence and power. Those who knew my father recalled his strength and wisdom.

*T*he degree of control that whites maintained over the reserves is made clear by the story my mother tells of her brother Harry's death in 1942, and the authorities' refusal to allow the family to attend his funeral. In order to leave the reserve or travel back there, Aboriginal people had to get a clearance from the reserve officials. This clearance was known as a permit. The permit system was standard procedure which operated from the Queensland reserves' inception in 1887 until the 1980s. Leave from the settlements was only granted in special circumstances for employment contracts, errands to other settlements and towns, medical treatment and, on occasions, funerals.

To Aboriginal people, the deep religious and spiritual significance of funerals places a huge onus on relatives and friends to attend these important events. A funeral is viewed as paying final respects to a worthy and cherished person. No matter whether the deceased was a close relative or community acquaintance, attendance is unashamedly commanded. Being one of the most honoured etiquettes of Aboriginal society, attendance may number in the hundreds. Absence at Aboriginal funerals does not go unnoticed, particularly if it is that of a close relative. Non-attendance therefore is largely scorned and considered an insult to the deceased and all surviving relatives.

My older brother Harry died when he was twenty-two years of age in Maryborough. He'd been working and was accidentally shot. We never knew what really happened. We were told it happened when Harry was cleaning his gun, then we heard it was when he was dingo shooting, but I think there must have been more to it than that. Mama cried every night at sundown when she heard. The houses had sticks to keep the windows up and when the sun went down Mama's wailing would be heard for hours through the open windows. We cried, too, at seeing her in such grief.

I remember my parents desperately wanting to go to Harry's funeral but the officialdom declined them a permit. I fretted to see them so hurt about it. Dadda made several attempts to go in his sulky but was refused by the superintendent. Thinking back on it, I wonder if it may have been punishment to him for his past behaviour. If denial was intended to hurt, it achieved just that.

While we had nothing materially in our childhoods on the mission, we were rich in other ways, rich in spirit. For us kids, there were always ways to be happy. I remember us making dolls out of bottles and cars out of rocks. We would go walking, fishing, hunting and camping inside the reserve. We were one of the few lucky families in Cherbourg to own a horse and sulky. That was like owning a Mercedes. But none of us was allowed to ride in the sulky without Dadda's permission and so none of us got to have a ride. It was used as transport mainly to and from Murgon which was about 5 kilometres away.

Murgon was the largest main rural town in the area. Other nearby towns like Wondai, Gayndah and Kingaroy were smaller places where the local pastoralists shopped. Murgon had all the modern-day things like a bank, post office, hotel, shops, railway station and when we would visit the town it was like exploring another world to us. Only non-Aboriginal people lived there then.

When we first arrived at Cherbourg all the children were sent to school. We'd never seen a school before. School was the place where we had the most contact with European ways. The lighter-skinned children would be separated from the darker children in classes with the idea of improving their learning. The teachers and missionaries were surprised when this did not happen. The dark-skinned children were just as bright as the lighter ones and some of the lighter ones were a few marbles

26

shorter than the dark ones. I always thought how awful that system was.

I first went to school when I was eight. There were two teachers and the principal, Mr Crawford, who'd give the boys almighty whacks with the cane. Auntie Janie Sunflower used to teach us at the school, too, and she'd take us for physical education, and play the piano-accordian and a mouth organ. It was nice to have one of our own people there.

Our room was a shed and in the front was the school office near the river. The school today is in the old 'top camp' area. At school there were about six European children in their starched clothes, the children of the white officials, and they mostly stuck close together. Sometimes we'd play with them but, I guess like them, we preferred our own mob. We never went outside the reserve on excursions to Brisbane like the white children and there was never any mixing with them outside school hours.

We used the old slates to write on. We were taught basic reading, writing, arithmetic, and a lot about European history, Captain Cook, and sewing. We were never allowed to draw or dance, which we were naturally good at. I don't remember the white teachers ever encouraging us to do things we wanted to do, or what we were good at. Instead, sewing!

As I've said, we were told not to speak our Aboriginal language, although we still spoke it out of hearing of the whites. We lost most of the Pitjara language, but we learnt Wakka Wakka words. That was the name of the local Cherbourg tribe. My brothers and sisters still know some words of that language. Although we can't speak it fluently anymore, the words we know are precious and carried on to our children and their children.

When I was twelve I was sent to the mission dormitory by the superintendent. I was very frightened. It was pretty rare to have escaped this experience for so long. I was put there as punishment for seeing boys. Just because we spoke to the boys,

27

the officials thought we were doing niggi niggi. A Black tracker came to our house and took me to the dormitory. It was because of Fletcher Brown, my first boyfriend. I would tuck scones under my calico bloomers to give to him and he would hide gingerbreads in his shirt. We had a puppy love relationship until he died when he was sixteen from tuberculosis.

The dormitory became home then. We were discouraged from thinking of our real home with our families. It did damage here but it could never sever the ties we had with our families. We were allowed visitors but my parents kept my brothers and sisters away in case they were kept in there, too. We were allowed to go home at weekends.

The dormitory was a two-storey wooden building with huge verandahs around it. It was near the teachers' residences. You could have eaten off the floors they were kept that spotless. An Aboriginal staff acting under orders of the superintendent controlled the dormitory routine like clockwork. Nancy and Charlie Chambers who were distant relations of ours were in charge of at least a dozen cooks, cleaners and other minders. Strict control and discipline were part of dormitory life. There was a range of chores to do such as making beds, washing clothes and linen in huge boilers, and scrubbing out the dormitory. We would go to school after breakfast and played after school. Then there were prayers, and dinner — mainly stew — which we ate in a huge dining room using enamel plates and cups. And then to bed.

It felt strange going to bed where there were three or four girls, not sisters. The boys were put into dormitories, too, but they were separated from us. The beds were lined up beside one another in long rows on either side of the room. My hair was completely shaved off because it was infested with lice. That was common on the mission.

I didn't like the dormitories but we deserved what we got because we didn't do what we were told. Sneaking around and talking to boys and all that business.

*N*o, *Mum, none of youse deserved it. They brainwashed you into believing you were responsible and it was your fault. It was about white paternalistic control and surveillance. Would you have sent us to a home? Even though you continually threatened us as small children, 'I'll put you all in a home if you play up'. I used to be terrified you would, so tried not to play up often — even though this never worked. No one deserves to be forcibly removed from their families.*

When I was thirteen, me, Betty Hart and Iris Hegarty were imprisoned for a week in Cherbourg gaol for seeing boys. Again, they thought we were doing niggi niggi, but we weren't. It was the only time I've been in gaol. We only had one blanket and one pillow and it was cold and we huddled together to be warm. It was so dark and scary in that place. They'd shaved our heads bald and gave us only bread and water. We never even had any munyoos. When they took us out, we had to do the housework at the dormitory, scrubbing the floors with our bare hands.

Unlike a lot of reserves we sometimes had corroborees. We would always go down to watch. Auntie Janie Sunflower would sit down and by just pounding a pillow she'd make this mellow sound which would blend with the other music. Women would sing but not dance with the men. Fires were lit by the traditional way of rubbing two sticks together. Men continued the dances and songs late into the night. The men were good dancers and would go down to Brisbane to dance for white people.

After school we would wander off to the local swimming place known as the Bogey Hole at Barambah Creek. In summer this place would attract the kids in droves, seeking out the cool water. Most of us would strip off and dive straight in. The boys preferred to climb out on the thick limbs of the tree and show off their different styles of diving. They all made sure that the girls they liked would be watching. Sometimes we would drift down on logs, splashing, singing and skylarking away. The younger children often came with us and it was our duty to look

29

after them. We might only have been ten years old but we were guardians to a bunch of babies. We would make sure that they had as much fun as we did. So much fun in fact that it became hard for us to get them out of the water. The older children would take them home whether or not they were their brothers or sisters. It was always like that when I was growing up. We had such a deep sense of loving for each other.

The Bogey Hole would also be used for baptism services by the Aboriginal Inland Mission. My brothers, sisters and I would sneak down on Sundays to see who was getting thrown back in the river. As we hid behind the bushes we used to wonder why everyone in the water was screaming and throwing their hands up in the air. We thought they must be drowning or something, but how could they be? Everyone knew how to swim on the mission.

Uncle Moses lived on the mission farm which grew many of the vegetables we saw but never had the opportunity to eat. Most of it went to the white officials. My friends and I would see him ploughing every day, going up and down the furrows with his faithful old horse and broken-down plough. Now, I had learnt my lesson well and good not to steal anymore but my friends had not. So while I stood guard and watched Uncle Moses doing his chores my mates stole the tempting vegetables. Sweet potatoes were the tastiest. My friends would take them home and give some to my mother who thought that Uncle Moses had given them to us.

One day I was not so quick. I was distracted and Uncle Moses caught my friends outright. He had a habit of waving a stick around and this time held it higher than normal and shouted to them to drop their loot. They hurriedly jumped through the barbed-wire fence where I was waiting on the other side. Uncle Moses was not fast enough to catch anyone and, as he ran towards us, someone called out something that our gang would remember for a long time and still rings in my ears today:

Moses, Moses,
when you die
your mundie closes!

G *rowing up in Cherbourg for my mother was a struggle and a* *privilege. There was an affinity and a cohesion between every-* *one. A Cherbourg experience has not yet been written which sheds light* *on the ever-growing success stories emanating from that community,* *in terms of Aboriginal activism throughout the country. Perhaps the* *younger generation has learnt many gracious and crucial lessons from* *their peers, for many Cherbourg descendants are now at the peak of their* *professions in Aboriginal community affairs such as Aboriginal education,* *legal and health organisations, and comprise large numbers in* *government and non-government positions.*

1. Chief Protector's Office, Removals Register, 1908–1936.

CHAPTER THREE

Servitude or Slavery?

F ROM THE END OF THE NINETEENTH *century through to the 1930s the effects of economic depression and drought and the resulting decline in the rural economy increased competition for employment. Relocating Aboriginals on reserves effectively removed them from opportunities to participate in an already depressed labour force. Instead, their labour was closely managed by superintendents and police who, without any consultation with Aboriginal people, arranged positions for them on the stations. In the late 1930s and the 1940s, control of Aboriginals' work was made law under the* Queensland Aborigines' and Torres Strait Islanders Preservation and Protection Acts of 1939–1946 *which empowered the minister, acting through a system of superintendents and police, to enter employment contracts on behalf of Aboriginal people, to hold any funds they might have had, and to supervise spending. The Acts essentially legislated a system of enslaved labour.*

From the 1920s to the mid '60s, the Aboriginal Welfare Fund held Aboriginals' earnings from their labours. No Aboriginals have ever seen that money. Some people believe that over twenty-five million dollars is owed. The government has responded to demands for the retrieval of these funds by saying that the money cannot be returned because the Fund's records are in such bad shape it would be impossible to ascertain to whom compensation should be paid.

SERVITUDE OR SLAVERY?

Aboriginal women were sent to work as domestic servants and nursemaids in station homesteads and in some cases as stock workers. The men performed stockwork and droving duties. This work began at thirteen or fourteen years. Domestic service was a cruel time for my mother, like so many women of her generation. The working relation was of the master–slave order. The men were addressed as 'Boss', the women 'Mistress'. Many women endured appalling treatment, including beatings and sexual abuse, and it was an experience that stood in gruesome contrast to the loving companionship they had known among their own people. Of course, there were some exceptions among employers, like Mr and Mrs Semple and their daughter Betty McKenzie. My mother still speaks of Betty McKenzie with great affection and regard. Betty continues to have associations with her workers and other Aboriginal friends to this day. That these white people treated their workers with respect at a time when this was so rare gives them a special place in the memories of women of my mother's generation.

Rita is reticent to talk about the regular beatings she received from one white mistress. I stumbled on this fact accidentally when a family friend told me of my grandparents' attempts to get Rita out of the way of that mistress before she killed Rita. My grandfather wrote to the authorities about my Auntie Ruby's conditions, and it is the most poignant letter.

Cherbourg
6/10/41

Chief Protector
Aboriginals
Brisbane

Gentlemen

Kindly oblige this Particulars matter & I have Girle Way this Three years and Some Part of Southfrook Ruby Holt She had Bad time at the Start With those People and she Not allowed Write to us & so I Want my Girle returne to

34

Cherbourg at once and hoping you Will returne her to
Cherbourg Without faile I wont have that Woman [to] have
her any longer that Woman wrot to Super here Said She
Was too young for the Wages first 12 month She Was there
so Hough Wont let her come home & So I Want Ruby Holt
come Home Want See her What State She in

Gentlemen oblige Without faile

yours faithfully
A. Holt

His letter received the following reply:

7th November, 1941

Albert Holt,
C/- The Superintendent,
Cherbourg Aboriginal Settlement
Via Murgon

Regarding your letter of the 16th October, you are advised
that from information received, your girl, Ruby Holt, is in
satisfactory employment and probably does not write to you
for some good reason.

It is not proposed to take any action to remove your
daughter from her employment and if you desire any further
information on this subject you should see the
Superintendent.

The Superintendent,
Cherbourg Settlement.

My mother does not want to talk even to me about the kinds of bitter treatment she experienced. I respect that, but I will not forget nor forgive the people who inflicted that pain. These events should be exposed so that we might have another view of Aboriginal labour history than the gross distortions that present those years as a golden age. However, I cannot speak of those years for my mother. What stops Rita speaking about them herself is not unusual — it's the same thing that stops other people speaking about profound suffering they have experienced. The oppression and pain can be so fierce as to make people mute. They close this experience inside themselves and don't want anyone to touch it. I will not force an entry but I have done my damnedest to get inside her pain, short of breaking down the door.

Guilt and shame are manifest in women who have suffered like this, and there is a self-blaming that makes them see their situations as their fault, or the fault of their race. They feel that they have gotten themselves into this mess, and are responsible for finding ways out. The sense of guilt will remain as a terrible weight to be carried all their lives unless they can allow themselves to challenge it and speak it. Women of my generation are freer to express our anger and pain because now there is a more general acceptance of the right to speak about child abuse; it's politically correct to address the maltreatment of Aboriginals; honourable to elaborate my oppression as a Black woman, etc. Still, Aboriginal women have to find our own ways of speaking about these things. The healing time can begin then.

When children were sent out to work it was never discussed with the parents. They were just told, 'Rita is going to Charleville next week'. The superintendent sent two Black policemen to get me down to the office. He gave me an order from the store for a dress, pullover, sandshoes, pants and bra, to look respectable I suppose. Officials never cared how Aboriginal people might feel. They just came and took us away for our sentences. We were like spare parts for cars, things to be used when needed, replaced when necessary.

I remember the expectation on all the girls that they fulfil roles as domestic servants. We had no choice where we went or what we did. My first job in 1934 was with a pastoralist family at Barcudgel Station via Charleville. Their huge living quarters was on a cleared block of land which was surrounded by bush and sheep as far as the eye could see. My contract with them was for twelve months after which I was sent to work for a policeman in Charleville. Sergeant Corbett worked with a Black tracker, Jack Mack, who I got to know along with his wife Mary. We were not allowed to mix together but it was good to know that there were other Aboriginal people around.

My first job was from dawn until the late hours of the evening, a daily routine of cleaning, washing, ironing, preparing food and caring for the children. It was a job I would do for the rest of my life. It is my background as a domestic that has in many ways shaped my whole life. Even today I do not feel comfortable and a whole person unless the day has been spent in some kind of domestic activity, whether it be cooking, cleaning or washing.

I would also milk and feed cattle and take care of sheep. Some young women would do fencing, cart water, cut cane, do droving and shepherding — they were jills-of-all-trades. Like my friend Annie 'Topsy' Hansen from Lake Nash. Her working days started when she was employed by a white family at eight years old. She worked as a boundary rider, drover, cook and many other things. She moved around with station work in the huge Aboriginal camps along the rivers.

We were always given the children to look after, bath them, change and wash nappies, but we were not allowed to discipline them in any way. This was one of the hardest things because some of them were so cheeky. But sometimes out of sight of the mistress and master I would take my revenge and quietly smack my spoilt charges on the bunthie. The days were long and tiring and never changed. All my day was spent helping the white people. At the end of the day, we'd have to eat in separate rooms out of sight of the family.

There was no more schooling for me. I was only thirteen but they thought I'd had enough education. There were no holidays either, and very little time for myself. My own chores like washing and sewing my clothes would have to come before I could go horse-riding and walking on days off. If I ever had some time to myself I'd jump on a horse and ride for miles and miles. We could all ride horses good. Or I'd go down to the creek, although it was pretty mucked up by the cattle. You couldn't eat the fish or drink the water because they do their business anywhere, those cattle.

Being so young I'd always get homesick. I would write to my family when I could. My daydreams and spare moments were spent longing for home. So much of girls' young lives were taken from them. We didn't really have a childhood like you think of it now. White folks had the expectation that it was their God-given right that we would work for them, and the experience of years spent in that kind of servitude took away a lot of our childhood and adolescence: playing, knocking around with kids of our own age. We were made to act like grown-ups and to have

Annie 'Topsy' Hansen
with Nellie Brown
at a station close to the
Queensland–Northern
Territory border, c 1910

grown-up responsibilities before our time. Child slave-labour in many ways.

We grew up so quickly in those days. This is probably why I expected my children and grandchildren to grow up fast through their early teens. When I was growing up there just didn't seem to be a period between being a child and an adult.

In some cases Aboriginals were denied permission to attend their people's funerals while in domestic service. My friend to this day, Agnes Williams, was not allowed to go home even for her mother's funeral in Cherbourg. She cried and cried and was broken hearted and has always felt cheated about that. I really feel for her. Her family shunned her for not attending because they thought it was her fault for not coming home. She was caught in a hopeless situation. If she dared run away or went on unauthorised leave she'd be sent to gaol. I heard about people who'd got caught trying to get back to their families. They got prison sentences for months and then when they got out they were sent to stations even further out as a deterrent. But it didn't work, because they still kept running away.

The balance of the small income we earned was withheld by what was then the Department of Native Affairs. The superintendent would 'look after' our money in departmental bank accounts and would regulate our withdrawals. I would be able to keep only two shillings pocket money from my weekly ten shillings pay. In 1947, Agnes Williams received a cheque with her exemption from the settlement for nine pound and five pence. That was all there was after ten years domestic service.

The great passion for all us girls was clothes. When we were little we'd watch the older girls return to the mission after their stints as domestic servants and they'd be clad in clothes that seemed so exotically beautiful to us. They paraded up and down the dusty streets of Cherbourg looking so elegant, tall and slim. We looked forward to the time when we could dress up like them but we didn't realise then what we would have to go through before we would experience our first taste of a little personal luxury.

'Boss' Semple worked as the superintendent in Cherbourg for many years. When he bought a house in the Brisbane suburb of Indooroopilly, his wife Matron Semple asked me if I'd like to come to Brisbane with them and work for her. I didn't hesitate because the Semples were very good to me while I was on Cherbourg. They were held in high regard by many Cherbourg residents. Their daughter was especially liked. She had a fine respect for Aboriginal people. There always have been a few committed and sincere non-Aboriginal people. We still love her. She is always on the invitation list for our Aboriginal functions, like the Golden Oldies which is held annually and brings together all the residents and ex-residents of Cherbourg. We have the time

(Left to right) Rita Huggins, Superintendent Semple, Wallace McKenzie, Mrs Semple, Miss George, Jack Denelin, Willie McKenzie, at Cherbourg c 1937 (courtesy McKenzie collection)

of our life reminiscing, laughing and telling tales about the olden days. Betty comes along with many of her Aboriginal friends.

When Betty married Wallace McKenzie, Mrs Semple suggested that I went to work for the newly married couple. So I was like an inherited domestic. Betty and Wallace were both very kind and always helping people. Wallace was a proud father and loving husband. I considered myself very lucky to have such nice people to work for. They spoilt me in lots of ways and gave me a freedom that I had never had in domestic service before. The respect they showed me I certainly felt for them, too.

In later years, I would visit them. But it was different then. They waited on *me*, with lovely cups of tea and homemade biscuits while we reminisced about old times and enjoyed our fond memories.

(Left to right) Rita Huggins, Jimmy Holt, Elizabeth McKenzie, Indooroopilly, c 1948 (courtesy McKenzie collection)

During my domestic service my first-born Marion (our name for her is Mutoo) was born in Cherbourg on 18 May 1942. Due to my young age and domestic service duties I left her in my parents' care. It was a hard thing for me to do but with being sent out to work all the time I had no choice. My parents raised my daughter as if she was their baby girl and considered her to be their youngest daughter. She had a strong bond with them and they gave her enormous love and support.

Mutoo became a grandmother herself at thirty-three which in turn made me a great-grandmother. Her eldest daughter Rosie gave birth to my first great-grandchild when she was young also. Now Rosie has become a young grannie herself at thirty-three. Harold Jr, who we call Bally, still lives in Cherbourg with his family and the youngest of Mutoo's family Tita (real name Desma Rita) and family live in Brisbane. I'm very proud of the fact that even though I didn't raise my daughter, she and her children remain

Marion (Mutoo), Cherbourg, 1960s

very bonded to my family. They know all their relations and stand together.

They always rally together for celebrations and sad times. And although the relationship may not be as close as my other children who I grew up, which is understandable, there is still a deep feeling of love, respect and loyalty to my daughter. She has the warmest, endearing personality and, like me I guess, loves all people of every race, colour, creed or class. People are attracted to her like a magnet because of her sincerity and outgoing nature and friendliness.

In 1946 when I felt that I was able to take care of myself I wrote a pleading letter to the Director of Native Affairs for my exemption. I had known some of my friends had done it, so I got game myself. You had to prove that you were able to make a go of it in the wide world.

Mutoo

43

SERVITUDE OR SLAVERY?

'Greenrigg'
Taringa Parade
Toowong S.W.1

Dear Mr OLeary:

I am writing to ask you, if I could have my excemption please. I am quite sure I will be able to look after myself. I have my eldest sister Margaret, whose had her excemption for some years now, she can manage quite well so I am quite sure I can also.

Violet has hers too, and I want to out and have a change of a place at any time I want too. I have been with Mrs Semple for 2 years now, and am quite happy and like her.

I will feel more happier if I was out like my two sisters and contented. I hope it won't be long, in looking into matters, and hoping to hear from you quite soon.

I Remain,
Yours Faithfully
Rita Holt.

A form came back, called 'Report on Application by Aboriginal or Half-blood for Exemption from the Provisions of the Act'. The questions were nosey and insulting: what was the 'breed' of my parents; 'does applicant habitually associate with aboriginals'; 'does applicant live in a civilised manner'; 'is he (or she) intelligent enough to protect himself in business dealings'. It was filled in by my boss, Mr Semple.

I did receive my exemption papers, and then I was free to leave and travel wherever I wanted to go. I didn't tell anyone where I was going because I was pregnant again and in those days it was a scandal to be an unmarried mother, especially now that I was considered a respectable and 'free' Aboriginal woman. I wanted to get out of Cherbourg and Brisbane because I never had the courage to tell my parents, especially my father. It was a shame job in those days to have two children before you were married and I didn't want to inflict any more pain or embarrassment on my family.

The thought of anyone finding out terrified me as I believed that I could still be sent back to the reserve life, and not be able to go anywhere. I would again have to face the restrictions and controls, so I did the disappearing act.

I boarded the train to Mackay to find my friend Lear Barber who had since married her new husband Ted Ram Chandra. Ted is a famous man who has had two books published about his life and now there is a movie in the making. He's called the Taipan Man and handles many venomous snakes. He's had a love affair with snakes all the time I've known him, doing many shows around the place and visiting remote Aboriginal communities. Ted has received many awards for his mostly unpaid work. He has played a vital role in helping the Commonwealth Serum Laboratory to develop an antivenene for the fatal Taipan bite.

I knew Lear first during the war when she and her family were evacuated from Thursday Island to Cherbourg. There was a threat that the Japanese might invade Australia from the north. Darwin had already been bombed. Along with other people who had to leave their homes, the Barber family stayed in the dormitory at Cherbourg. Lear's sisters Supia and Sadie soon became my friends, too, as we were all around the same age. Granny Marion Barber was a wonderful woman and mother and I named my Marion after her.

After crying on the train all night, I arrived in Mackay. I asked a cab driver whether he knew where Ted lived. As it was a one-horse town in those days and not the big place it is today, I figured people would know each other and I was right. He drove me to North Mackay where I was warmly greeted by Lear who introduced me to Ted. I asked them if I could stay a few months with them and they replied, 'Of course. You are family, Rita'. I'll never forget their help and hospitality. I never told them I was pregnant, only that I was looking for a job. However, I couldn't fool old Grannie Barber who took one look at me the next day and nodded knowingly at my tiny stomach while the others weren't looking. She never said a word to anyone until I confessed some months later when my pregnancy was becoming obvious.

Lear's younger sister Sadie and I were pregnant at the same time and ended up in the Mackay Hospital in 1947, each giving birth to a girl. My Gloria June (after my friend June Bond) was born on 20 August. She was a cute and cuddly baby who everyone loved. Sadie and I would push our girls in their prams into the town regularly for the exercise and to get rid of the boredom.

I had not seriously looked for a job in Mackay because I was pregnant but now was a different story. On one of our trips into town I went into a chemist and asked the people working there if they knew of any domestic jobs. They put me in touch with a Dr Grant who I went to see immediately at his surgery with my Gloria in tow. I asked him for a job on the condition that I take my baby with me. He agreed and I started work for him the next day.

He had a beautiful home within walking distance of where I lived. I'd get up very early in the morning, dress Gloria, feed her and then tidy myself up, ready for a full day's work. The work entailed mostly housework and cleaning. Mrs Grant would do all the cooking and offer me many home-baked cakes and biscuits to take home. They both were very good to me and I suspect that, in their own ways, they felt sorry for me as a single mother.

I stayed in Mackay for three years until my homesickness got the better of me. My mother was constantly on my mind. I missed her a lot and felt guilty because I never wrote her any letters. When I had made up my mind to return home, I thanked my good friends for having me stay with them. I had a little money behind me now and the sense of security that gave me made me feel more confident that things would be all right in other ways, too.

In 1949, when I got back to Cherbourg with my little girl, Mama ran out of the house to embrace us in a tearful reunion. Even though I didn't correspond with her she had heard through the Aboriginal grapevine that I had given birth to a baby girl. She brought Mutoo out to meet her new sister who affectionately hugged and kissed her. Luckily Dadda was away hunting because he was still angry that I had had another child out of wedlock. He never spoke to me for a long time and let it be known that I was not welcome in his house because he considered me a disgrace to the family.

I had no choice but to sign myself into the girls' dormitory where I stayed with other single mothers. There were many young women who had just returned from domestic service who had recently given birth or were pregnant. This was common. I met up again with many of my old school pals who were now young mothers, or about to become mothers. Some already had a few children.

I can just imagine what it must have been like in your time to be a single mother, not once but twice. Single motherhood is a hard and unrelenting job but the love for the child and all the worthwhile outcomes far outweigh the difficulties and courage needed to be alone.

But as a single mother I have never been alone in the sense that you were. My anchor and the ability to do what I have to do, write, speak, travel etc., comes from the fact that primarily you and Ngaire share the responsibility of being a mother, carer and nurturer to John Henry. It has been an unconditional act of love from both of you and I am so privileged to have been born into a culture and family so accepting of children and family.

You were hardly more than a child yourself when you ran away from your family to a strange town where you only had two friends.

SERVITUDE OR SLAVERY?

Luckily Auntie Lear and Uncle Teddie were family, loved and cared for you as best they could and gave you a desperately needed home in your time of need and your highest form of being.

I saw not only the loving way you welcomed my child into this world when I was confused and so unsure myself what the responsibility of being a mother might mean, but I also have seen the radiant way you welcome into the world all babies — of strangers as well as of the closest friends and relatives — and the way you welcomed particularly your grandchildren and great grandchildren. I understand so much more now.

I'm sure Mutoo realised that you had to go to work. You had no choice in a life of domestic service. You were bonded and on contract. If you could have taken her out on the stations, you would have done so but in working from daylight to dawn there would have been no room for a small baby. Today we have the right to take our children with us to work. No one would dare take them from us.

For me, being a single mother has meant independence, freedom, choice, acclaim, unreserved happiness, status and power over my own life, among other things. All of which you were never afforded. But things we shared in common were love, strength, stubbornness, struggle, shame in the beginning, absent fathers of our children and, most importantly, being broke! Financial independence has to be worked at all the time but still I have a far greater capacity to achieve this than you ever could have dreamed of in your day.

All I want to say to you is that it's okay. All your children and grandchildren love you, understand you and forgive you because being a single, Black and penniless pregnant woman in your time was your greatest test and punishment.

Report compiled by Rita's employer at the time of Rita's application for exemption from the Aborigines Protection Act (courtesy McKenzie collection)

SERVITUDE OR SLAVERY?

Place _Brisbane_ 8R/35₉

Date: _18_ _11_ _46_

Report on _Rita Roef._

Hired by _Mrs Rumple, Taringa Parade_
Indooroopilly

Date of Inspection: _13 . 11 . 46_

Employer's Report re Progress, Character, and Behaviour of Child:

No complaints

Child's Statement regarding—

Food:

Treatment: } _Is very happy._

Accommodation:

Pocket Money:

Condition of Child as to—

Cleanliness of Dress and Person: _Neat & tidy_

Health: _Good._

Contentment: _Yes._

Accommodation: _Room in shed near house_
fairly well furnished. This will be
Outfit: _(improved later on_
when building
becomes easier)
Appears sufficient &
suitable

Workers' Compensation Policy Renewal Receipt ___ No. ___ Date

Nature of Work performed: _General Housework_

Pocket Money Book: _In order_

Religious Duties:

Remarks:

_3/4/12/46_

J. McAntehrson
Inspector.

SERVITUDE OR SLAVERY?

JUL 1946

No. 85

"The Aboriginals Preservation and Protection Act of 1939"

REPORT ON APPLICATION BY ABORIGINAL OR HALF BLOOD FOR EXEMPTION FROM THE PROVISIONS
OF THE ACT

: MURGON :

Questions	Answers
Name of Applicant	*Rita Holt*
Sex	*Female*
Age	*23 years*
Where born	*Spring Sure*
Breed of parents –	
Father	*Half Caste*
Mother	*Half Caste*
Were parents legally married?..	*Yes*
Is applicant married (legally)?	*No*
If so, what is nationality of wife (or husband)?	
Does applicant (or his family) habitually associate with aboriginals?	*Visits parents or Boggimual*
Does applicant live in a civilised manner and associate with Europeans usually ?	*Yes*
Applicant of good character, steady in employment, and industrious?	*Yes*
Does applicant drink	*No*
Or procure it for other aboriginals? ..	*No*
Is applicant educated, to what extent? ..	*Yes. State School*
Is he (or she) thrifty, and does he (or she) understand the value of money? ..	*Knows value of money. Red. is not. Yes if have good.*
Is he (or she) intelligent enough to protect himself in business dealings? ..	*Yes*
What amount has he (or she) to credit or debit in the Savings Bank?	
Has applicant previously been granted exemption?	*No*
Remarks:	

RECOMMENDATION OF PROTECTOR:-

(State whether exemption is recommended. If so, whether from all provisions of the Acts, or only in part. In latter event, state provisions which should remain applicable.)

This Girl has a Child aged 3 years, but Grand Parents will take Care of her & little Girl.

Signature

Employer's report, 1946 (courtesy McKenzie collection)

50

FOUR

Summertime

I FIRST MET JACK HUGGINS in 1940 when I was working in Brisbane as a domestic servant. Ten years later when I was twenty-eight I met this tall and handsome Aboriginal man again at the Boathouse. The Boathouse was a popular haunt for us then. Every Thursday the Aboriginal girls who worked as domestics in Brisbane had their pay, and would go down there. It was mostly Aboriginal people and we danced — old-time waltzes, pride of Erin, foxtrot. It would often hold a couple of hundred people, and squeeze even more in on a good night. There was a huge verandah at the back where lovers could spoon, hold hands and talk. Many love affairs developed there among my friends. Mine was no exception. The Boathouse was down in William Street, where the expressway is now. The trees are still there. I go there now sometimes with my friends and sit down where the Moreton Bay fig trees are.

Jack (John Henry the Second) Huggins lived in Ayr in North Queensland. He was a 'free' man and enjoyed his life to the fullest in his home town. His life was a direct contrast to mine. He was never put on a reserve and he basked in his freedom which showed in his confidence and equality to non-Aboriginal people. As with all good-looking Black men, Jack attracted white women to him in droves. He had a string of white lady friends chasing him, but it was this little black duck who eventually won his heart. I fell head over heels in love with him and have never known a love like him. I will always love him until I die.

Jack would come down from Ayr every couple of weeks or so to see me, and he'd write to say when he was coming and when to meet him at the railway station. And I did. I was happy having a boyfriend coming all that way on the train from Ayr, North Queensland, to Brisbane to see *me*. It would always be a Thursday we'd spend together. There is a park in George Street with a statue of Queen Victoria and we used to get behind that and hold hands and kiss. And this went on and on for months. We always finished up at the Boathouse in the evening.

One time he asked me to meet him on a Wednesday instead. At that time my mistress and boss were Mr and Mrs Hood. He was a bookmaker, and worked on the Brisbane turf. I asked Mrs Hood if I could have Wednesday off instead of Thursday, and Mrs Hood said, 'What's the special occasion?' I said, 'Oh, I've got a boyfriend, and he's coming down from Ayr'. She said, 'I knew you must have had a boyfriend. You going off all the time'.

This Wednesday night we went out to dinner and he gave me some flowers. He grabbed me by the hand and he looked into my face, and I sort of looked away and he said, 'Look into my eyes. Will you marry me?' And I cried. I said, 'Are you sure you've got the right girl?' And he said, 'I'm sure I've got her now. When I leave you I can still see your face'. He was so romantic. He put the ring on my finger. It was two hearts. And my wedding ring — this little band of gold — it never leaves my finger.

Jack wanted to meet my people. I asked Mrs Hood if I could have the weekend off, and she said, 'Yes'.

When I took Jack up to Cherbourg, Dadda was out. Mama said, 'Who's that mardie? What did you bring him up here for?' And I said, 'Mama, I'm going to get married'. She said, 'You be a good wife to him if you get married and give him children'.

Mama had made eight dampers. They were on the racks to cool. She always cooked one for an old woman who was even poorer than my mother. Jack looked at these dampers and said, 'Oh, Rita, I've never tasted damper for a long time'. Mama, poor old thing, she only had a pot of stew and rice but Jack said, 'That's the best meal I've ever had'. Mama was lovely.

My father came back. He'd been having a game of cards. He looked at me and he seldom laughed or smiled but when he saw Jack and said, 'Who's that mardie?' and I told him we're going to get married, he smiled then. He took me into the other room and said, 'You be a f. good woman to him'.

Jack and Dadda disappeared, then, into a room by themselves. I had no idea that Jack had brought three bottles of beer and a bottle of rum. Mama said to me, 'Where those mardies?' and when she knew what they were doing she said, 'Shut the doors and windows. When anyone knocks, don't open the door. We sleep'. When Jack came out, I told him he had been lucky that he wasn't searched when we came onto Cherbourg. Alcohol was not allowed. He could have been put in prison rather than being with me.

He was not allowed to stay overnight, but he did anyway. We had to have permits to get on and off the reserve, even to visit our families. To make matters worse, we would have to pay the authorities to accommodate us! It was like booking into a minus minus minus five-star motel. This is the letter I had to take with me on that visit to Cherbourg:

19th July, 1951

The Superintendent,
Cherbourg Settlement.

The bearer, Rita Holt, and her daughter Gloria have been given permission to visit the Settlement for the week-end in order to see Rita's family.

She will be accompanied by Jack Huggins whom she states she is going to marry. It has been made clear to Rita that Huggins will not be allowed to remain on the Settlement over-night.

All expenses of the journey will be met by them and no cash advances are to be made.

Deputy Director of Native Affairs.

I never met Jack's people. They had died within months of each other when Jack was away in the war. Jack's mother was known to have Maori heritage but I could not find out much about his parents. I believe they were a very proud and dignified couple. Jack was broken-hearted when his good friends in Ayr told him of the bad news on his return home. They hadn't been able to trace him for a long time and it was believed he was killed in action. But, thank the Lord, John Henry Huggins came marching home into my arms. He had been a prisoner of war on the Burma/Thailand railway and found it hard to speak about his experiences there. Jack respected his mates who had served with him and would love to frequent the RSL club to mix with them.

*M*y father's father, John Henry Huggins, who had fought in World War I at half the wages of white soldiers, married a woman we have always believed through family and local Ayr community ties was Maori. Some of the uncles and aunties on my maternal side have always told us our father was Maori and an only child. One of my aunties used to remind us that we weren't Aboriginal, but Maori.

Fanny Huggins, my father's mother, was born Fanny Constantine at Fort Constantine in Cloncurry, Queensland in 1886 to Lizzie Constantine. Unfortunately there is no father's name listed, which must be the Maori connection. Aboriginal and Maori babies were never registered at birth so I have to rely on my second 'oral-tradition' skin to further track my great-grandfather down. Sadly, most of the old people in Ayr who knew my grandparents have passed on now, but I am confident that I will find someone to talk to. The search continues to find my Kuia (Maori grandmother).

My sister Ngaire was given her Maori name by our Kuia long before my father ever considered the likelihood of having children. We often call her Ngio and Ny Ny for short. I was named Jacqueline which was shortened to Jackie after my father in case he never produced a son.

In August 1993, I attended a conference in Aotearoa, New Zealand, where I was graciously greeted and welcomed by some Maori sisters, and I told them that I had had a Maori grandmother. I didn't feel at all that I was being fashionable, claiming Maoriness under false pretences, the strategic use of the 'other' for convenient alliances but, hopefully, to find a clue to my Maori family. One of my Maori sisters, Teremoana Sparkes, gave me the greatest compliment by replying, 'Yes, I know. I can see it in your eyes'. My mother has always told me I have my father's sad eyes, that can sear through a person's heart. It would be more genetic than anything else, I suspect.

It has often puzzled me why my father's family stayed in Ayr and remained 'free' people while other Aboriginals were being herded off in droves to the missions. Did they claim another identity in order to stay? I deny this emphatically and it depresses me even more to think this was true. My own uncompromising identity politics couldn't stomach it, but I can understand my grandparent's generation trying to survive and keep a certain amount of dignity intact. There would be no excuse for it today. Then, to be anything other than Aboriginal meant higher status, more power over their lives and escape from the mission concentration camps. My father's family certainly would have been exceptional in their time, having quite egalitarian relationships with the local white townsfolk who recall my father and grandfather as true gentlemen and my grandmother as a dignified lady.

Now people around the world are rushing to find their indigenous ancestry when once it was a real shame job. It's been found that even Elvis Presley had Cherokee heritage. I never believed it would happen in our country, people wanting to find their Aboriginal ancestors and *all, and I'm surprised to hear that it is happening. Strewth, I'd better go into an Aboriginal genealogy consultancy business. It'd pay more than writing books!*

Jack and I were married in 1951 in a small ceremony in front of thirty people at the All Saints Church, Wickham Terrace. I wore pink and Jack was more handsome than I had ever seen him look — the blushing groom. Our reception was held at the RSL Club in Wickham Terrace and our honeymoon night at the Railway Hotel.

Rita and
Jack Huggins

The next day we caught the train to Ayr where I was going to live now. We had a week's honeymoon on a huge cane farm called Rita Island, some 20 kilometres west of Ayr. There was nothing particularly flash about it except it was owned by some of Jack's friends who had known his parents. So Rita Holt became Rita Huggins and honeymooned on Rita Island.

Ayr was a vibrant little town and I liked the way it smelt of the sugar cane and I liked its friendliness. Italians and Kanaka people worked in the town in large numbers. I could not recall many Aboriginal people. Well, I guess I mean Aboriginal people who looked like me, straight-haired and binagurrie. There were many who had South Sea and Aboriginal mixed heritage but we all called ourselves Murries. Our colour and lifestyles brought us together.

Jack was well known in Ayr. Not only was he a keen sportsman but the first Aboriginal man to work in the Post Office in Queensland. A then-young Shereen Malamoo would always tell the story of how she and her sister would proudly amble up to the counter and bump each other on the shoulder, requesting the purchase of a stamp from him. 'Hi, Jack! How are you today?', they'd call out loud like big women in the hope that everyone was listening. They felt so proud to know a Black man in such a powerful position. And, yes, in those days it was a rare sight to see and it was a big deal, not only for them but for all the young kids there. He was a role model for them and could prove that there was another future in the district other than cutting cane.

Shereen Malamoo is now a well-known woman in Aboriginal affairs. She is also a fine jazz and blues singer. She used to sing that song *Summertime* to my children while they were young to get them to sleep. That song was so true. The livin' was easy, fish were jumpin' and the sugar cane was high! I hear her still singing that song all over the place.

My husband's love of sport and the odd drop of ale kept him regularly entertained with his male friends. In his younger and fitter days before the war he was an A-grade footballer and lifesaver. He had many loyal mates who would lay down and die for him because of the charismatic person he was. He introduced me to his wide circle of friends, who readily accepted me because I was Jack's wife. That was the greatest honour. We were so happy together.

My second daughter, Gloria, was eight years old when Jack and I married. Jack loved her as his own. Time was flying past and I wanted to have my younger children quickly to my husband as I was then in my thirties and felt time was running out for all of us. So then along came two more girls — Ngaire and Jackie — and a boy, John. This felt like a complete little family.

(Left to right) Jackie, Gloria with John, and Ngaire, Ayr, 1958

One day in hot summer we went to visit some friends who lived on a cane farm. The girls were little and Jackie, who was always the yunjilbai one, wandered off into the cane fields. I swear I had my eyes off her for only a few minutes but it was time enough for her to disappear. I pity all parents whose children have accidents when they so much as turn their heads because it happens so fast. When I realised she was gone I screamed out to Jack and our friends who began to search the hundreds of narrow cane fields. A small, eighteen-month-old baby could get lost forever in those rows. I felt my stomach turning as we searched and thought we'd never find her. We sang out to no avail.

A while later, just as we were about to give up, this little voice came singing through the cane, 'Hey, diddle, diddle, doh!' There she went, thrashing a piece of sugar cane to either side without a care in the world. It would seem my young daughter didn't know about all the fuss she had created. She also had a gudja guna for me to fix up.

Jack and I were outside one day, doing some gardening. Gloria, Ngaire and Jackie were playing outside as well. We had a big, old, lemon tree which Jack was pruning. Jackie was sitting on a blanket not far away when the branch fell and the thorn went in her head. We got it out but she sobbed for hours. She was born with no hair and the mark was noticeable.

It wasn't as devastating as another time when she and Ngaire were attempting to do some gardening. Jackie was hosing and Ngaire had a huge hoe, tapping away. As usual, Jackie was annoying Ngaire to the point where Ngaire warned, 'If you don't get away, I'll hit you with this'. Jackie was acting binungunj as usual. The next minute I heard a scream and there was my girl with blood streaming all over her face. Jack acted quickly and put a towel around her head and we rushed her up to the hospital. She had seven stitches and still bears the scar in her head. I always told her she's got a hard head.

Some of our dearest friends were Stan and Hilda Mitchell and their children. We met them soon after our wedding in 1951. Jack was in the garden when he saw Hilda who was pregnant and pushing a pram with some of her other children. Hilda says Jack was the most handsome man she'd ever seen. It was a hot day and he invited her in for a cup of tea. We've been friends ever since. Hilda and I had an instant liking and have seen our children born and our husbands die. It's this bond we share and she is my best friend. We go back forty years. She was a young mother as I was then. New to this country, Hilda came from England and I welcomed her to Ayr by being friendly to her.

Christmas Day would be spent together, with Jack and Stan enjoying their Christmas cheer. We had barbecues together and Sunday School picnics at the beach. We had an old table-top truck that all the kids would jump on the back of. In those days overloading was no problem. We'd putter off to the beach at Rita

The Huggins family home, Soper Street, Ayr

Island and the kids would go berserk in the water and sand. It was ever so wonderful.

We had magical times in Ayr but little did I know that I would only have seven beautiful years with Jack before his health began deteriorating. Jack became a permanent fixture in the Ayr Base Hospital. He suffered a stroke and lost some movement in his arms and legs. The doctors told me his war injuries were contributing to his ill-health. I faithfully visited every day with the kids on my waist and in prams. Jack's illness was long and he was too sick to be aware that we finally had a baby boy after all the girls. John Henry Huggins the Third was just four months old when his father died in November 1958.

Due to war injuries, Jack required some attention from specialists in Brisbane. Nana Evans lived at Murrarie and I stayed with her when we came down to Brisbane while Jack attended

Jack in Ayr

Greenslopes War Veterans Hospital. As the children were playing Nana looked into the lounge room where I had put Jackie on the floor. She was only nine months old then and crawled in her unusual way — on her bottom, with arms outstretched on either side. All of a sudden she jumped up and took off walking. She walked so soon in life and being a determined Leo I knew she would succeed in life. We laughed so much that day. And that's the way Jackie always crawled, on her backside. It's very unusual to see a child mobile like that but as she got used to it, she would dart and dive around the house. People would come to visit just to watch her.

A beautiful old lady who befriended me and helped me in my time of need was Granny Liza Lampton. It was hard to tell her age but when she died it was said that she was well over one hundred. Her slight build and snow-white hair belied her vivacious personality and huge heart. She was a kind and well-respected lady who was born on the banks of the Burdekin River and was a clever woman.

My next-door-neighbours, Teddy and Betty Roe, came in late one night in November 1958 with a message that the hospital had rung to say Jack was ailing fast. Granny Liza was with me at the time and hurried me up, 'Quick, you better go to Goobra (her name for Jack)', she said. I walked up to the hospital, hurrying alone in the dark. When I got to Jack's bedside, Canon Thorpe was there saying prayers and I sat down and prayed, too. It didn't dawn on me that Jack was dead. I reached out to touch him, and it was only then that I realised. He had died from a massive heart attack and he was only thirty-eight.

When I returned Granny Liza was waiting up for me. I said, 'You know?' She nodded and pointed to the clock to the precise time — eleven o'clock — that he passed away. She could not read or write.

Jack had the biggest funeral. I had no idea my husband was so respected in a little town called Ayr. Just recently I found out he dived into a swollen river and saved a man's life. It was just like him to do that.

I still have some dear friends there who were with me during the time I lost my Jack. Some have passed on now like my wonderful friends Eileen Lampton and Val and Sam Johnson. Eileen's large family and their descendants still live there and I am particularly fond of Norma and Desley who remember the trauma we all went through when Jack departed this earth.

The little house we owned still stands. To see it brings back flooding memories of the fabulous times we used to have and the sacred love I hold for Jack. Here we started our family who were born in the Ayr Hospital. His whole life revolved around his home town.

My dearest father had died needlessly due to a war which he had no control over. More than this he was not yet a citizen of his own country but was considered good enough to go to war. While his people were being denied the basic human rights, for example education, he wore the patriotic uniform of the Australian soldier proudly. I had often wondered why he loved the army when the hypocritical society in which he and my mother lived in that time was brainwashing our men into believing they were equals, when they did not even have the right to vote or to be counted as Australians. Maybe if Dad was alive today he'd be able to tell his children, who hold uncertainty about his motivations and anger at never knowing their father.

More than anything my children felt deprived of having a father and to lose him through the war injuries he received didn't seem fair. He never recovered in his head from his trauma which is why I guess he never spoke about the war. Only on one occasion did he mention that some of his fellow soldiers, before their capture as POWs, shot and ate a jungle monkey because they were starving. Jack internalised a lot of pain and anger about that period of his life and was never able to share any of it with me. I wish he had.

There have been men in my life since Jack. I was so lonely after he died. But I would never meet anyone to match him and have never remarried. For to have married would be to say goodbye to Jack completely and I could never have lived with that. He is always with me in spirit. I think and talk about him every day.

CHAPTER FIVE

The Grand Experience

I CAME TO BRISBANE IN 1959. It was closer to my own country and to my family. Ayr held too many memories for me, I saw Jack's face everywhere. With my four young children, I moved to Inala, a Housing Commission area in an outer suburb of Brisbane. We were one of the first Aboriginal families there. Inala is an Aboriginal word for good camping place by running water, and the place always did have a very Aboriginal sense about it. I could see them in the old days living there, sitting around the campfires telling the stories, singing and dancing. Now Inala has the highest population of Aboriginals and Torres Strait Islanders in Brisbane.

Being in a city was very hard for me at first. Looking back, I think that the changes I went through at that time were too big. Without Jack, and in a new place, I felt very lost. I was grieving beyond belief for my precious husband. My life felt like one big, empty hole with no way to climb out. I was very angry that Jack had died and wasn't with me and our children.

I had very little resources for raising a family all on my own. The only job I knew was domestic service. But it was impossible when three of my children were under three years of age. What money there was came from Jack. He had always been a good provider, and he was able to support us after his death as well.

He had contributed to a superannuation fund from which I received a small fortnightly cheque, as well as a war widow's pension from Veterans' Affairs. This money was a godsend and enabled my family to have shelter, food and clothing.

However, I didn't always use the money in that way in the first years after Jack died. My grief swallowed me up and I looked to things that would take me away from my cares. I loved to go out at night and let my hair down. Actually, in those days I wore it up in a beehive. I spent money on good times and alcohol, and sought relief in the friendship of other men. I just wanted to have a good time — anything away from the grief.

I spent a lot of time at The Grand Hotel in Mary Street, down by the wharves. It was a concrete pub with a small, shabby lounge and a public bar. Many Murries used to meet there. People from all parts would come together to catch up on news of friends and relations. Every Friday and Saturday night The Grand would come alive to the beat of the juke-box and the hum of voices filling the dimly lit, smokey rooms. Women would sit on the men's laps and, while chairs were scarce, the laughter and beer were not. It was a place where everyone felt like one big family, fights and all, and boy-oh-boy, were there some fights.

In those days there were plenty of 'captains' who were willing to share drinks, smokes and their company with us. But they didn't get it all their way because sometimes we'd beat them at their own game. The power for once was in our court until we tired of it all, then we'd leave. They'd get gooly up, but who cared? Lonely old guys, too, would wander in from the streets into the Murrie pub where they knew they'd be listened and spoken to and given some respect, if they deserved it. We'd even give them taxi fares home. A lot of younger Murrie women were also regulars at The Grand. When the ships came to town the sailors would be buzzing around and I don't think they could resist the temptation. Someone must have told them about us. As they told me later, The Grand was important to these young women in their growing up. They learnt to deal with a society that was very different from their own. Something of their identities as young women was formed at The Grand, as well as some streetwiseness and the ability to deal with hungry white guys.

It was here at The Grand that I met one of the loveliest people in my life, Harry Hapameni, a merchant seaman from Finland. Harry would stay at our place on his weekend leave. We'd all go for bush walks and picnics which Harry just loved. I could have easily fallen in love with him, but what was the use? He would soon be going home to Finland and I would never see him again. I was an Aboriginal woman and could never leave my land for anyone.

Betty Hart and Rita, Brisbane, 1965

The way in which relations between women worked was very interesting. We'd always be loyal to each other and defend one another, but when it came to a man two women wanted, it would be every selfish thimbun for herself. One day a woman I used to call a friend pulled my hair down the toilet because she was jealous of her date's attention towards me. Betty Hart was my best friend and backstop at the time and came to my aid. Betty had been a school pal at Cherbourg and could out-fist the boys any day — a real tomboy. She was well known as a good fighter and would put off any bully. I always felt safe around her. If anyone hit me, she'd take it up for me and bash him up. We had a lovely sisterly friendship all our lives. Betty never had any children but would spoil my children as if they were her own. My children loved her very much in return.

Although she was very protective towards me, I sometimes hated going to the pub with her because she would get jealous if her boyfriend so much as looked at or spoke to another woman. Her round, black, red-lipped face was scarred by fights and if

The
Grand days,
1968

a white person who she didn't know so much as glanced at her she'd say, 'What the f'n hell are you looking at? Haven't you seen a Blackfella before?' She got worse when she'd had a few drinks. She was such a wild woman. Everyone was scared of her.

Betty changed in the 1970s when she found the Lord. She became a committed Christian, involved in full-time Church work. I was so happy for her. I saw that gentle side of Betty that I knew so well begin to outshine and take over. She began dressing better, really looking after herself and had a special glow about her. Betty remained a loyal friend until her death in 1986.

*M*y mother had much loyalty and generosity towards her friends. It wouldn't be rare to bring them home to sleep. They'd always be women though and sometimes we'd get a fright to see another person sleeping in our room on a mattress on the floor or to have our brother or sister in bed with us while the friend slept in one of our beds.

Although we had only a little ourselves, we still shared whatever we could. Mum would usually feed her friend the next morning and then send her home in a cab. She felt sorry for them because sometimes it would be the only feed they had had in days. She collected all the strays and brought them home like the caring person that she was.

We never winced about this, though, because Mum seemed to get a lot of satisfaction from this. Besides, her friends were always nice to us and gave us a few bob if they had it, which wasn't often. We called them all Auntie and even today they acknowledge us fondly. One time, Auntie Caroline Doolan wanted to take me out to the Birdsville Races with her boyfriend because I was her favourite. Needless to say, I never saw Birdsville. Actually, a few of my aunties promised me many things which I never got. They were so loving to all of us which made up for lots.

Little did I realise how in those days I was neglecting my children who began to suffer. I usually left them in the care of my second-eldest daughter Gloria who was only in her early teens herself. I think now what a burden and huge responsibility it was for a young girl to take care of her younger sisters and brother when she should have been the one who was going out all the time. I don't know what Gloria had felt about all this because she never complained — not to me that is. She may have to her friends but she was such a beautiful and generous spirit who was kind and understanding to everyone.

My children told me much later in their lives how they were hurt by my not being there. How my priorities were solely about me and my life. I was so busy having a good time that I'd spend most of our money on drinking and socialising. My children paid the price, but I couldn't see it. As long as I was having fun, who cared?

Yes, Mum, I hurt a lot about the bad old days but they are gone now. Writing about them has proved an extraordinary healing process for me and I'm sure you won't mind me telling a few yarns.

I remember when I was eleven, and wore that scungy old green seersucker dress constantly to school until it was in tatters. One day, this freckly, skinny, smart alec schoolboy asked, 'Don't they stock those dresses in other sizes or colours?' Ngaire was into recycling at an early age and would mix and match two outfits to go around for as long as she could. And, well, Johnny just didn't care, did he? He had a persistently runny nose and needed hankies more than clothes. Neither did we have any shoes and would walk to school barefoot. However, in those days many of the other kids in Inala hadn't shoes either so it didn't seem to worry us. Can you imagine your grandsons doing that today? It would be a real shame job, ey?

Vegemite sandwiches were the norm for lunches and some days we were so broke that you'd wait until the bank opened on pension day before you could take our lunches up at recess. Our hungry little faces would faithfully greet you as you handed the lunches over the fence. 'Thanks, Mum', we'd appreciatively say and scurry off. As soon as that 'motherly' duty was performed you'd get done up perfectly and rush off into town. You were always immaculately decked out like a queen, with dress, jewellery, handbag and shoes all matching. We'd just sit and watch you. Everyone commented how great you looked and, being a real Leo, you just loved the flattery.

I can still see Johnny, who was about nine, over at the local Commonwealth Bank agency withdrawing twenty cents for some margarine. I think there was only about fifty cents in the account anyway. The shop assistant must have felt so sorry for him because she ignored the withdrawal and gave him the money out of her own purse. We can laugh about that now.

I realise now why my daughters give their children everything. It's because they missed out on such a lot of material things in their time. They can't bear their children to go without while they have the money. Sometimes I criticise them for spoiling their children as I think it's healthy for kids not to get everything they ask for. But I can't blame them because they know the real meaning of being poor when they were young and what it is like to go without.

My spending went on for years. We always seemed to be broke except on pay day and it would be gone again in the following few days. To tell the truth, I never knew how to budget. We had very little to spend anyhow and Jack had always handled the household money. I never learnt the value of money and how to make it last until the next pay. It was in one hand and out the other, all in a matter of days. I'd get so excited the day before pay day and never really plan how to spend it. All I knew was that soon I would be having a good time. My fortnightly thrill was coming up and I would look forward to the next one. I didn't understand hire-purchase either. It was a quick way of getting goods like fridges and washing machines without much cash. So I would sign up. Soon I found myself unable to keep up the repayments. I would hide in my room when the bill and rent collectors came around. They would get abusive to my children when they told them Mum wasn't home.

Spending on the wrong things meant I couldn't keep the roof over our heads. Rental arrears began to mount up. I had no one to blame except myself. One cold July day in 1969 a Housing Commission rent collector caught me at home when the children were at school and served an eviction notice. My kids were angry with me when they realised what was happening. We were going to get evicted from our house and not only would they lose their home but their school and friends as well. They never forgave me for that. It was a huge disruption to our lives. A long series of moves around Brisbane followed. If I'd known what would happen I would have paid the rent, arrears and all. For years we didn't have a real home anywhere, just temporary, seedy, accommodation to look forward to.

We moved to the inner-city area where times were tough. I got in boarders, one at a time. The kids didn't like having an extra person but it helped with the rent and food. One star boarder was old Frank who must have been eighty years old and still working. He was bald, toothless and had suffered a stroke years ago. He had worked as a carpenter all his life and would cause his employers some fright because he refused to give up work. He'd travel up to eighty miles a day to work. All he had was four weetbix for breakfast and I would pack him sandwiches for lunch. Poor old Frank was never any trouble to me.

I remember one slack week, we had nothing in the house to eat — no muntha or anything. Johnny the animal lover had a pet duck called Harvey that used to roam around the yard, just minding his own business. My brother Oliver was staying with us and was used to having his meat at night. As there was no meat I had no hard feelings in baking up Harvey for the evening meal. Oliver loved it but all the kids could do was to stare down at their plates. They had put two and two together. Suddenly Johnny jumped up and said, 'Where's Harvey?' The next morning

with tears and bookah streaming down his face he went outside
to pick up the scattered duck feathers.

*I*t's been very hard for Rita to talk about these days. In fact, I know
you don't like to be reminded of them, do you, thimbun? I
believe these are the hard years that have added and made you the person
that you are today. No one is perfect, as you've always told me. You
need not feel ashamed anymore.

Despite the hard times we had, all of us would say that we had
a beaut childhood somehow. Sure, we'd complain, off-load and fight
because they were ways of relieving our anxieties. It was probably our
closeness as children which gave us the security and love we felt so
deprived of at times. But insecurity and loneliness weren't even issues
because we had each other and, besides, you always came home to us
in the end. You could have told us all to get nicked and put us in foster
homes but you chose to keep your children and we love and respect you
for that.

My mother blames herself for those years, but they are not problems
that were peculiar to her, but ones common among Black urban
communities. Aboriginals in Brisbane were not only faced with the
difficulties of being newcomers, but they were dealing with a cultural
shift from the reserves or rural areas and small country towns to an
urban area. Aboriginal people had been moving to the capital cities,
because of greater employment opportunities and greater freedoms that
emerged after the war. With freedom from the reserves came the unlocking
of rights that had previously been completely unattainable for them but
that had been taken for granted by non-Aboriginals: freedom to move
around the country without permission, to earn a wage and keep it,
the prospects of jobs and education, a chance for a life over which we
had some control and, most important of all, the freedom to express
oneself. Not all Aboriginals who came to the cities liked the life or were
able to find work, but a significant number stayed. By the mid 1960s,
approximately one in every five Aboriginals lived in the capital cities,
a dramatic increase on the pre-war period. It has been estimated that
about five thousand Aboriginals lived in Brisbane by 1965.

THE GRAND EXPERIENCE

Most white Australians would have had no knowledge of what my mother's generation of Aboriginals faced in the shift to the cities. White Australians knew virtually nothing about the places my mother's people came from except for some ill-conceived notions derived from the media. It was, after all, the days when the practice was strong of taking children away from their families in the name of protection. The myth abounded of Aboriginal degradation, hopelessness and inferiority, part of the collective unconscious of the white nation. While the most violent acts of persecution of Aboriginal people were usually confined to the more remote, frontier regions, nevertheless racial prejudice and discrimination persisted in the cities.

It wasn't uncommon, for example, for Aboriginal families to be forced to lead a life of urban itinerance, moving house perhaps four or five times a year, because of the attitudes of white neighbours and landlords who had no tolerance of Black ways. So, for instance, offering a place in our homes for transient or homeless relations and friends was (and still often is) viewed with great intolerance by whites. It was expected of Aboriginal people living in cities that they undergo huge cultural change, conforming to white ways.

There weren't many Aboriginal people living in Inala in those days and poshy white people especially were very backward in their attitudes and understandings of us. And today not a lot has changed in that respect at all. I have heard many stories from my people of how they get discriminated against by real estate agents, by lawyers, by doctors, and the ways they get treated by bus drivers and taxi drivers, and by people in shops and hotels. It happens all the time.

I remember the time when my children were little in the '60s, Johnny got a rash on his arm. I took him to a local doctor who took one look at me with my three other children in the waiting room and, when it came my turn, said, 'You're Aboriginal'. I wasn't sure if it was a question or a statement. I thought how strange it was for him to say that. I told him my son had an itchy rash on his arm. He didn't even bother to examine my child but said right away, 'He's got scabies. I'll prescribe some lotion which everyone in the house must use and you'll have to wash all your clothes and bed linen'. It didn't feel right somehow but I went home and did exactly what he had told me, even though none of us other than Johnny had the rash. A week later Johnny still had it. A friend took one look at Johnny's arm and said it was an allergy of some sort and I should take him off dairy products for a while. Two days later the rash disappeared. He'd been cured and I'd been conned!

What could I do? I'd been taught to trust and respect doctors, people in authority. I wasn't confident enough to challenge him. Perhaps today it would be a different story because I have had heaps of experiences with doctors and other health people who have tried to pull the wool over my eyes. I would now demand a proper examination, or get a second opinion if I didn't feel satisfied. Just because he had seen a lone Aboriginal woman with a mob of kids in his surgery he presumed that we were dirty.

In the years after the war, Inala was a dumping ground for migrants and thousands of people with nowhere else to go. It was no wonder that Aboriginal families would find their way there. I suppose it was like Elizabeth in Adelaide, or the western suburbs of Sydney. When we moved there in the late '50s, it seemed that mostly everyone was a battler, gunin gunin. The crime rate was not as bad as it is today. We were all so poor, Aboriginals and whites. It didn't matter what colour your skin was. Some of the whites were worse off than we were, and that was saying something! Public transport didn't exist, and without a car you felt pretty lonely. Some of my nephews had old cars they'd done up and they would take us for drives.

I didn't have a car then and used taxis when I had to. That's how I met my good friend George Hodges and his family. He'd taken me into town from Inala in his taxi one day in 1964. We struck up a good friendship and I liked him so much that he became my personal chauffeur (at a price) for the next ten years. Sometimes the kids and I would get bored and we would tear off to the Gold Coast or up to see my mother at Cherbourg in George's taxi! When Mama first saw George she said, 'Who that withew?' I said, 'He's our taxi driver, Mama'. It didn't take long for Mama to like him. George was a tall, well-mannered man who was reliable, honest and a damn good taxi driver. My children liked him a lot, too. He was a good friend to me. His children were about the same ages as mine and on weekends my children would stay with him and his wife at the time, Rae. They spoilt my children rotten. It was nice to know such lovely people.

One time, Johnny must have been feeling lonely without a father because he always had his mum and three big sisters nagging him. He proudly asked, 'George, will you be my daddy?' George's face went red and he nearly died on the spot but couldn't refuse those big brown eyes. 'Yes, mate, I will.' Johnny called him Dad from that day on.

*W*hen George's taxi pulled up, we would get so excited because we knew we'd be going on a long trip. Mother would usually prepare us well in advance for the destination and while we loved going to the beach we'd baulk at Cherbourg because it was a long, hot ride for five hours. This trip was pretty monotonous and we'd anxiously wait to get there as fast as we could, and play 'I Spy' all the way. I'd usually win because I cheated by changing the object every time someone guessed it.

On arrival in Cherbourg our Gran would hug, kiss and greet us warmly. She never knew we were coming. We just turned up, which is always the way with Aboriginal families. No formal phone call or message needs to be given that you are coming. You just turn up. Everything gets accommodated. While Grannie would take us inside and give us cordial and biscuits, George and Mum would get a cup of tea. George would automatically lie down in a bedroom after the long *and noisy drive. He was such a gentleman and I can never recall him telling us to shut up. Mum did that quite handsomely, come to think of it.*

I often recall those days and how strange it must have been to see an Aboriginal woman and her back-seat load of children being driven around everywhere by a white taxi driver. George didn't seem to mind, though. He had enormous respect for my mother and perhaps, in his own way, felt a little sorry for us, too.

During our Inala days I didn't see as much of my brothers and sisters as I would have liked. They were all so busy with their families to rear. Barney, Oliver, Jimmy and Lawrence worked on the railway all over the place. Sometimes they'd come to visit and stay with us. Barney and Dolly, Oliver and Myrtle and families were the ones who visited the most.

Barney and Dolly would come down from Aramac where they lived most of their life. Barney would drive all the way. He was a good driver. Dolly loved to play the organ. Some years before my dear sister-in-law passed away she bought an organ and would play it all day. She was a card, dear old Doll. Lillian and Peter, their daughter and son, were always coming home to visit me.

Oliver, Myrtle, Rhonda and Rose always came down from Central Queensland to go to the exhibition in August. Around that time, the footy finals were in full swing. Oliver was the biggest fan. He'd love to go. Myrtle was good company for me while the girls enjoyed seeing each other as well. Rhonda came to stay with us when she went to Business College. We would visit Oliver and family when they lived in Capella, Clermont and Dingo on school holidays. The kids loved it. It was something different for them.

Margaret and Major lived in Eumundi where Major worked on the railway. Jimmy and May lived and worked in Gatton at one stage. We'd visit them sometimes too. Isobel lived up north.

Thelma and Clare lived in Cherbourg. Later some of them moved to Inala, but after we had left. Albert and Marlene still live there.

Ruby married George Martin from Stradbroke Island. They lived at Piimpama and we'd get in our taxi to see them. Ruby would usually make a mulberry pie and custard. She was a great cook. It was beautiful.

There were only a couple of other Aboriginal families that we knew of in Inala at that time. They were the Bond and Kirk families. I knew Hughie Kirk's family from Cherbourg. My late friend Freda Kirk was a gentle and gracious woman and I miss her very much. She was great friends with my daughter Gloria. Luckily we just lived down the road from them and they were always coming to our home. My children, who could be the biggest myalls, would hide under the beds from the Kirk kids, too scared to come out. However, this didn't last long. They went to school, played sport together and to this day remain firm friends.

There was a very special relationship between my family and my late dearest friends Nuggett and June Bond and their family. I consider all their children nieces and nephews, and my children have always called them cousins, although they are not blood relations. I grew up with June at Cherbourg and she was my closest friend. One beautiful thing about having grown up in the reserve is that we were one big family even though we came from different parts. We shared experiences, and we shared our families.

Auntie Rosie was a regular visitor to our house. When I met her she had just come back from Scotland. She was a nanny there. Some white people had hired her to work for them. It was so unusual for an Aboriginal person to go outside her country then.

Auntie Rosie was the most gracious person and the best cook I had ever met. Dumplings were her best. She stood almost five foot nothing and had the cheekiest grin. The dimples in her cheeks lit up her beautiful face. She'd always come over with food and something for the children in big bags. She came and stayed weekends while she worked as a domestic during the week. Her working relationships went on for many years. She was well respected and loved by her employers.

Her daughter Barbara was Gloria's best friend. They shared so many things together. I knew Glor confided a lot in Barbara. Barbara works in prison education now in New South Wales. Auntie and I went through teenage-daughter problems together. So we stuck together like glue over lots of things.

*A*untie Rosie and I shared a bond of friendship so much that I loved her like my own grandmother. Our faces would shine when we saw each other and hugged. She was a generous and wonderful person with a humanness unparallelled in most people I've met. She taught me many things about life and told me some stories about the old times. She took a special interest in me and hopefully I reciprocated her warmth. I wish I had listened more intently to what she told me. Instead I was easily distracted as a child and wouldn't listen to anyone. Her knowledge was vast. She was well travelled and spoke her language from western Queensland fluently. In retrospect, I believe she was attempting to pass on information which she knew as a tribal woman. If only I could revisit those days, sit down, listen, talk, ask questions and write it all down. I know I would have been a better person for it. I love you Auntie Rosie, rest now.

We Murries played many a card game in Inala. As early as I can remember on the missions our people have played cards. It is a way of spending time together, but I think today cards have been abused too much in certain places and can be seen as a gambling habit. It can be an enjoyable activity if it's used in moderation — like all things. Some would-be winners would come over to our place at the weekends and do their dollars something terrible. Mind you, it happened to me as well so we were only sharing our profits between each other. The outright winner would leave wearing a grin from ear to ear while the rest of us suffered in the wake, wondering where we went wrong. 'If only I'd had another ace or something', they'd say. The grin would only last a week and then get fairly wiped off at the rematch the next weekend.

U s kids loved the card games, too. So did my nieces and nephews who'd come in for free hands if we economically blackmailed them into making us a cup of coffee or if we went to the loo. The magic of those intense days are good to reminisce about and it was good for their schooling, too. The games had an educational component to them since they were good mathematical tools. Many an Aboriginal kid has learnt to count and perform simple problem-solving exercises before they went to school by the process of cardiatricks — which way.

Inala has always had a reputation. Now, the large number of people on welfare, unemployment, crime rate among young people, the fights between the Vietnamese kids and Aboriginal kids and, no doubt, its high population of Aboriginals and Torres Strait Islanders, all attach stigma to it. But there always was a determination in the people to succeed, particularly among the kids. I know it was the case with my children. They were proud to come from Inala. A lot of the problem is Inala's isolation and the boredom that exists among the kids. The people are workers when they can get a job.

Despite the hardships, there has always been a spirit of cooperation and friendship among many people in Inala. Even today when we drive out there to visit relations and friends we recall the good old days. I've always felt proud to have lived in Inala, along with my children who hold a very deep respect for the place. It was our first home in Brisbane and I loved that little house. Even though it's not our home anymore the great memories can never be replaced. The friends made there will never be forgotten although some have moved on to other areas.

But most of the kids who grew up there remain to rear their children. Or they stay in nearby suburbs close to their old home.

The Queensland Premier Wayne Goss comes from Inala. His father was the local barber. Everyone who's ever lived there says, 'Wayne Goss's father cut my hair'. Well, he'd be a millionaire twice over if he had cut every person's hair who has claimed so.

We moved to The Gap in 1972. It's so leafy and an attractive area. Some friends Peter and Adele Kerridge had a fifteen-acre farm at The Gap which they asked me to look after while they were transferred to Malaysia for three years. I jumped at the chance because we had moved around so much and it would give my children longer stability. Johnny was the only one left at school then. It was a glorious place. The house was small but comfortable.

Peter said, 'There's a cow to milk', and I said, 'Oh, yes, I can milk the cow' and we had chooks and we had ducks and a big dam where the kids swam and there was a boat. We thought we were rich. Rich. But it all belonged to Peter and Adele.

CHAPTER SIX

The Natives Are Getting Restless

T HE 1960S BROUGHT WITH THEM *some very exciting years of protest that helped bring Aboriginals' concerns into the public view nationally. One of the first protests was the struggle by Doug Nicholls and the Aboriginal Advancement League of Victoria in 1963 for the Lake Tyers Reserve which the Victorian Aboriginal Welfare Board wished to close down in pursuit of its assimilationist policy. On 22 May 1963, Nicholls and forty Lake Tyers residents marched to state parliament and petitioned for retention of their reserve.*

A year later, in 1964, the Foundation for Aboriginal Affairs was formed in Sydney, which carried out important welfare work among Sydney's Aboriginals. Indeed, the Foundation, which worked in opposition to the Aborigines Welfare Board and often most effectively, gained the financial support of the New South Wales government. One of the Foundation's founders was Charles Perkins, organiser of the Freedom Ride bus tour, primarily comprising university students, throughout New South Wales in 1965 to highlight the continuing discrimination against Aboriginal people living there.

Traditional people also protested in the 1960s. In 1963 the Yirrkala people sent a petition on bark to the House of Representatives. They protested at the excision of some of their land for use by the bauxite mining company, Nabalco. *The petitioners claimed that they were never consulted, and that the land which they still used in the traditional way was vital to the livelihood and independence of the Yirrkala people. The importance of the issue and the claims made by the Yirrkala people forced a parliamentary investigation. Although the select committee did not accept the need to cancel the lease, it made the historic recommendation that compensation in the form of either land grants or money must be made for excised land.*

In response to a similar injustice — the Arbitration Commission's decision in 1965 to delay equal wages for Aboriginal pastoral workers until 1968 — the Gurindji people walked off the Wave Hill pastoral station in 1966. This strike soon developed into a land claim. The Gurindji people sent a petition to the Governor General that the area around Wattie Creek was sacred and that their forefathers were killed in the early days while attempting to retain it, and therefore the land was morally theirs and should be returned to them. The Yirrkala and Gurindji disputes were important landmarks of change and developed into crucial symbols of the Aboriginal land rights struggle. With all this energy happening it was no wonder Aboriginal people were excited and hopeful.

The 1967 Referendum was also looming. A 'No' vote would brand Australia racist in the eyes of the world and would also be a slap in the face for Aboriginals themselves. Of course, the Referendum was not a question of politics but of human rights and human equality. The 1967 Referendum resulted in constitutional changes that established the long-overdue mandate for the inclusion of Aboriginals and Torres Strait Islanders in the national census and at the same time gave to the federal government concurrent powers with the states to enact legislation dealing with Aboriginal affairs.

Rita in these years was actively involved in the One People of Australia League (OPAL), a Queensland-based organisation begun in 1961 in Brisbane. Branches were later set up all over Queensland. It was founded by Muriel Langford, an Englishwoman who had been a Christian missionary in India. She had read an Australian magazine showing Aboriginal people living in great misery. When she questioned an Australian friend about the Aboriginal people she was told that we couldn't hold alcohol and anyone who supplied us with it was sent to gaol. In 1956 the Langfords migrated to Australia. They firstly went to Tasmania where Muriel was told there weren't any Aboriginals left. A year later the family moved to Brisbane where she was told that Aboriginal people live way up north and that she wouldn't meet any in the cities. This invisibility struck Muriel. She felt a loathing of Aboriginal people by whites that she had never experienced anywhere else in the world. As a Christian she wanted to change the situation and make the world a better place, one in which Blacks and whites could co-exist in harmony and equality.

Because OPAL was founded by whites and had many prominent white members, it was often criticised, and still is, for being a conservative organisation. It didn't go along with the more revolutionary approaches, since these didn't necessarily feel right for all Aboriginals, especially at that time. OPAL wanted to begin organising around important issues without attracting even more hostility to Aboriginals. Many Aboriginals were still afraid of authority. Only the brave ones would become involved in Aboriginal activities. Some Aboriginal people felt inferior to whites and were worried about what the whites would say about them. Murries were already on the outer and didn't want to be further out.

OPAL also has been criticised as being assimilationist, following the government policies of the day. The policy of assimilation was hypocritical when the Queensland government made it near impossible for Aboriginal people to live as equal members of the Queensland community. What kind of possibility for assimilation was there, especially for those Aboriginal people whose only experience was on the missions? OPAL, instead of assimilation, spoke of integration, rejecting the idea that Aboriginal people desired to live as white Australians did. Assimilation policies didn't recognise the worth of Aboriginal culture and ways of life. They didn't see how important solidarity and community are to us, and that we must reject some white ways for the sake of our own survival.

85

One thing that helped me in those years at Inala was my work with OPAL. OPAL gave me the strength to survive my problems, and to try to help others who found themselves in the same boat — my own people and poor whites. For over thirty years OPAL had been a major influence in my life. I worked as a director of the organisation for twenty years, and am still a life member.

OPAL was for people like me who no longer lived on reserves and had moved into the towns, and was a first step towards helping Aboriginal people. It gave the white people another picture of us that they had never seen before. We had always been out of sight and out of mind before that. We were decent people and this could be seen now. We were just as good as white people, but different to white people. It also brought Aboriginal and non-Aboriginal people together for the first time. We could be on the same level now without having a boss or mistress around. I began to feel like an equal. We became friends and socialised together. This was one of the most important parts of OPAL for me.

As an organisation we didn't want to be political and I liked it that way. We wanted to make the best of living in the cities, without having to bow down to anyone anymore. I hate politics and don't consider myself a political person, but my daughter says I am — was born political and always have been. Maybe I am.

We had a happy working relationship with white people. I remember the hours spent listening to them speaking. I was so impressed. They seemed to do it properly. I learnt a great deal from this. I have seen many changes in OPAL over the years and one change is in the relations between Aboriginals and whites in the organisation. In the early days, the white people would do a lot of the public speaking on Aboriginal issues. Now Aboriginal people get up and do the talking. We are more confident because we have become used to dealing with white people. In the early days our white friends in OPAL were also our teachers. I'm sure they get a kick out of seeing us as the

86

teachers now. They come to our community meetings and events and sit back and watch while we do the organising and the talking. It was this friendship between Aboriginals and whites that I enjoyed. I love all people of every colour, race and creed. There was never the chance to mix with others before OPAL.

There is more Aboriginal control and management in OPAL now, which is good. But I would like to see more whites in OPAL. OPAL is getting away from its original aim of Blacks and whites working together. I don't believe that because someone has a dark skin they should get the job. They should be qualified and do the job for our people and not for themselves.

OPAL was said to be an assimilationist organisation but I never believed this was true. Assimilation was a strange word to me. It meant that we should become white people, which I could never accept. I am Aboriginal and proud of it. Instead of being made to feel ashamed of our identity, OPAL strengthened it. Migaloos thought we would be better off if we could be like them, but they could never ever take our souls away and smash all the things that our parents had taught us.

In OPAL I was able to do things my way. I could use my Aboriginality as a force, without being made to feel shame. Many Aboriginal people were educated about the world and Aboriginal affairs through OPAL. The munyarl was finally coming out of us. OPAL gave us information. It put Aboriginal people in the spotlight. It was where Aboriginal people began to speak about their concerns.

Former senator Neville Bonner is probably OPAL's most well-known person. In 1945, he moved to Palm Island and became involved in Aboriginal issues. Later he became president of OPAL. In 1971 he was sworn in as senator and became the first Aboriginal in parliament.

OPAL wasn't the only organisation for Aboriginals in Queensland. There had been the Queensland Council for the

Advancement of Aboriginals and Torres Strait Islanders (QCAATSI) in the 1960s. Like OPAL, it had been started by whites. It was full of them in the beginning. Aboriginal people involved in the early days included my good friends Lambie and May McBride, and the late Celia Smith. Lambie (real name Stan) and May McBride were, and still are, a handsome couple. May was a short, neatly dressed lady and Lambie was a tall gentleman in a suit when I first met them at a Brisbane Aboriginal community meeting. May was the publicity officer and Lambie the president of QCAATSI. Lambie was also a strong trade unionist in the Waterside Federation and gained their interest and involvement in Aboriginal affairs around the time of the 1967 Referendum. May and Lambie were the prince and princess of Aboriginal politics in the late '50s and early '60s, and such a fine pair.

May and
(Stan) Lambie McBride,
1964

They were always with Celia Smith, who was also actively involved in community affairs for many years. Her family would possibly be one of the oldest Brisbane Aboriginal families. She would cook, organise funerals, and hold meetings — all unpaid work. She did a lot of work for Aboriginal people long before it was fashionable. Celia's sister Lucy Hutton was June Bond's mother.

There has always been Aboriginal people in organisations like QCAATSI and OPAL, caring for our people. Auntie Janie Arnold helped at OPAL House, a hostel for Aboriginal people in Brisbane run by Joyce Wilding. It was Mrs Wilding who first introduced me to OPAL. She was a long-time supporter of Aboriginal rights. Her work was dedicated to the welfare of Aboriginal people. She and Aunty Janie were always willing to give Aboriginal people accommodation and meals.

Auntie Janie has not changed her lifestyle since I knew her in Cherbourg over sixty years ago. Auntie Janie comes from Purga Mission near Ipswich. She has been cooking, washing, ironing and cleaning all her life, and she has reared many children. That was how I first saw her at Cherbourg, with children hanging around her skirt. She has the look of love for young children still in her eyes.

Auntie Janie is a magnificent elder and community lady. She never ceases to amaze me with her energy and concern for her people. She is at every march, protest, social function, meeting and conference and has been on many Aboriginal boards and committees, supporting and speaking up for her people. An inspiration to many people, she is a real fighter. Local Brisbane Murries love and respect her and she would know the family connections of most of them. She also makes no bones about the need for them to be accountable back to their community. This is a strength which I see lacking in a lot of our people today but it has been my good fortune to associate with the people who do this and are really committed to better changes.

It was a big thing in the late '50s and '60s to have been involved in organisations in the way these people had been. They offered years of effort and dedication to their people. At that time for so many Aboriginal people just surviving was a big enough effort. To find the extra energy for this kind of unpaid work was the most unselfish thing anyone could do. The government and other people did not trust people involved in Aboriginal organisations. Any organisation seen to be helping Aboriginals was said to be full of communists. I never really knew what a communist was but must have met a few in my time.

OPAL supported the 1967 Referendum. I remember the great excitement around that time. Our campaign was to persuade Queensland voters that they should vote 'Yes'. We began sending out leaflets to many organisations to give to their members who would send them to OPAL branches, churches and other services. We were finally going to become citizens of our own country. How nice it was for the British to grant my people that.

It was very good to see some changes coming to my people. That was one of the wonderful things of being involved in OPAL — I felt part of these changes. But there were other rewards too. In OPAL was the first time I remember ever speaking up and being heard by others. I was the quietest person then — believe it or not, my friends — nothing like I am today, never stuck for a word. In the old days I was new at the speaking game and thought people would put me down and say, 'Hang on, that's not the truth'. I was also scared to mispronouncing the *werd*. If I did, I would always blame it on my false teeth. I spoke to people who had never even known an Aboriginal person before. I would speak to them about my family, my people and our culture. I felt wanted and needed — and an Aboriginal diplomat. (Gamon!) OPAL gave us a community of support. It gave me a sense of freedom, responsibility, strength and, most importantly, helping other people.

Through OPAL, I wanted to do things that mattered and quickly. Being amongst my people rather than in board meetings meant more to me. My old friends held my interest in OPAL. My best friend Daphne Lavelle had also been involved in OPAL for many years. While housing, education and employment were among the organisation's major concerns I worked more at bringing people together. That was what I liked to do best. Without this work I would have felt very lonely at home. But as it turned out it was being with people — the talking and encouraging, and putting people in touch with others — that seemed to be where my strengths lay.

At OPAL we were able to keep the feeling of family going when people came to the city. One of my many jobs in OPAL was to help the Aboriginal people who came to the city from reserves and country areas. I would help them get in contact with relations, applying for housing and social security, and schooling for their children. There was a sense of being in this together, of being one people, and sharing whatever we could.

Perhaps it was because of this family feeling around OPAL that I felt responsible for the young people. I hoped to be a good influence and get them to trust me. There was a Younger Set in OPAL. It was a social club made up of the young members of OPAL. They were mainly teenagers who organised Christmas parties for the children, bus trips, dances and other things. Their first project was organising a ball on National Aboriginal Day. After its success, weekly dances were held. These young people would come to my house — OPAL's unofficial Inala office. They were comfortable there. I would welcome them with a hearty hug and kiss, and refreshments. On off-pension week we'd have Arnotts biscuits instead of the cakes and scones I'd make the other weeks. Decisions were made happily with no big noters taking the floor. This was best for letting everyone get on with the job. I also had the ability to make people feel comfortable in the most stressful situations, due to the way I dealt with people. I guess my genuine interest showed.

One thing I was very involved in was the children's holiday camps. The idea was that Aboriginal children and white children would have some contact with each other. City children went to the country, while Aboriginal children from the reserves and other country areas would come to the city. The camps began in 1961,

The visit by the Governor of Queensland, Sir Henry, and his wife, Lady Abel Smith, to the OPAL camp at Margate in 1968. Rita is seated between the Governor and his wife; behind her is Willie McKenzie; Iris Hegarty stands third right; Gretel Langford is kneeling, with camera. (courtesy Langford collection)

when fifty children came. Two years later this has grown to 140. Then up until 1972 there would be around 220 children. They mostly came from missions and settlements. The camps were for ten days, and the kids were left longing for more, but the organisers had had it by the end.

In 1964, over 100 children camped at the premises owned by the Methodist Church at Margate, and over 200 children from the outback enjoyed an exhibition week holiday in Brisbane. I remember this year well. We had many visitors at our camps,

Rita with the Governor at Margate; Celia Smith is the first woman on the left facing the camera; second on her left is Muriel Langford. (courtesy Langford collection)

and that year, Sir Henry Abel Smith, Governor of Queensland, and his wife Lady May accepted an invitation to visit. The aide rang Muriel Langford and said in a very superior voice, 'Their Excellencies will only stay for about half an hour'. But once there, they just wouldn't go. Sir Henry came down to the beach with us. There was a photo somewhere of kids hanging onto him at either side. He quickly organised races on the beach, and kept saying to his aide: 'Another two shillings, please, to give to the winners'. Little did he know that Aboriginal kids could run so fast. As soon as one race finished, another one started. The bungu got eaten up. The poor aide went round to all of us grown-ups when he was broke, begging for two-bob bits to keep the Governor going.

I had been asked to act as host to Sir Henry and stuck to him like a leech. Just as Sir Henry and Lady May sadly climbed into their Rolls Royce everyone sang *Now is the Hour* and our visitors had tears in their eyes as they left, and how were we to know that a few days later they really had to sail away far across the sea as the song says.

One year, all the media were there on the first day, filming away. Then in the evening the whole camp crowded round the TV to see ourselves. Will I ever forget that evening as we watched? As many of the children had never seen the sea before, the cameras wanted to catch them rushing into the sea for the first time. Johnny Huggins was the one who one lucky photographer had his camera pointed at. Into the water rushed Johnny and in his excitement let go of the pants he was holding up. Down they fell! What a scoop — the bare facts, as it were! The children roared with delight. We still laugh about that today. So, into town I raced next day to get him new togs with decent elastic this time.

As OPAL was becoming well known, a famous and very handsome TV personality, Ron Bray, rang up to invite us to take a number of our children to the Brisbane Royal Show — the Ekka — with TV cameras trailing. Of course, we were delighted at the extra publicity this would bring us, and Muriel said to me, 'Stick to him like glue, and bring the kids back afterwards'. Poor me! That was in the days of the stiletto heel, and as I was always up with the fashion my jinung nearly killed me. What a terrible day it was for me, though of course it was a thrill to go around the show with the famous personality, and have all the treats. The pace was furious but, as usual, we got good publicity. Aboriginal people were becoming very visible in those days, and OPAL was quite famous.

OPAL got into the media. The Aboriginal people had been neglected for so long, there was a lot of catching up to do. We knew the media could change what people thought about us. That was why we kept up the pressure. We had to make the most of every opportunity to be seen in a positive way. The efforts paid

(Top left to right) Sherrin (Doods) Murphy and Deeveena Murphy at OPAL camp, Brisbane, 1977 (other children unidentified)

off. OPAL still remains the most well-known Aboriginal organisation in Queensland among both Aboriginals and white people.

To raise funds, OPAL held an annual Badge Day during National Aboriginal Week in the second week in July. OPAL members usually sold the badges. In 1966, several members of the cast of *Uncle Tom's Cabin*, who had been contacted by OPAL, sold badges while dressed in their costumes. Branches sent badges to clubs and churches with the hope that badges would be bought by the members of these organisations.

All my children went in this event. They would gather on the corner of Adelaide and Albert streets in Brisbane, ready with red badges and huge, enticing smiles. They hoped a friendly passerby would make a donation to a worthy cause sooner or later. For the children, the day was considered a sickie and welcomed relief from school. However, they would be overcome with guilt when their classmates spotted them on TV and announced this in front of the teacher and full class the next day. After the fifth year of selling badges, they became bored and demanded some money for their hard work. I could only respond by giving each child one pound. They bailed up after that and the Badge Day fizzled out not long after.

OPAL has always been a very important meeting place for Murries. It organises all sorts of gatherings. The OPAL Ball is like a Murrie version of the RSL Girl in a Million Quest because we think all our young ladies are girls in a million. It is different to the usual European beauty quests because beauty doesn't necessarily come first. The entrants are judged on Aboriginal culture, current affairs, interests, ambition and hobbies.

The place where it is held is usually the flashest place in town, like the Sheraton or the Hilton. Everyone gets done up to the nines. Sometimes you don't recognise people as they walk past in their evening clothes. The dress is always formal, dinner suits for men and after-five evening wear for women — with no exceptions. I think our people love to do that for at least one night a year. I feel so proud to see everyone looking beautiful. We turn into Cinderellas and Prince Charmings for a night. However, these days it's usually me who turns into a pumpkin if we stay later than midnight. Once upon a time I could stay up all night but the ol' bones get very weary now.

The Ball is also a place where you feel comfortable about going without a partner. There are tables full of beautiful men and women of all ages who usually pair up by the end of the night. If this doesn't happen, there's always next year to look forward to.

The Master of Ceremonies is usually a well-known Murrie who introduces entrants for Miss OPAL. The show starts when the young ladies appear from behind the curtain. Then they answer a few questions for the audience and parade across the

Rita
with
June Bond,
OPAL Ball,
1973

97

room, like other quests. By the last one everyone has picked their winner for the night. It's better than lotto and just as sad to have only one winner. I have often thought how hard it is to be a judge. A local Aboriginal band, usually Mop and the Dropouts, plays in the background. By this time, the audience is on the third course of their meal. The winner is announced finally. Her family and friends sing out like they have just won the lotto or bingo.

The OPAL balls are still going strong. 1990 was the most packed I've seen it for many years with about 300 people there. I had to laugh because the National Aboriginal and Islander Day Observance Committee (NAIDOC) Debutante Ball was held a few months back and that too was packed to the hilt and they say we are having a recession at the moment. But that's nothing new to Aboriginals because we are always in a recession. Many who attended the Deb Ball came to the OPAL Ball as well, so many good times are still to be had in these lean times. It's nice to know that we are not the only ones suffering.

Our annual debutante balls are inherited from the reserve days. They are a great form of entertainment that I think began around the time that Queensland Aboriginals were getting politically active in the late '50s or early '60s. It was a time that Aboriginal people felt a bit freer and out of the clutches of the government officials. It was considered that young people, particularly young women, were coming of the age to enter the outside world. The young women dress in white lace and long gloves. My daughter Gloria and her daughter Sherrin made their debuts in Cherbourg about twenty years apart.

When we have balls like these, my thoughts wander back to my late dear friend Caroline Archer who did so much for the Miss OPALs. She was a wonderful lady and a strong supporter of Aboriginal rights. She took charge of the OPAL balls every year to make them the huge successes that they were. Her organising talents, along with Billy North's, could not be faulted. Billy's a permanent fixture as a judge. Billy owned a modelling academy and would encourage young Aboriginal women who looked like making it into modelling. She was interested in Ngaire at one stage but Ngaire had other plans for her life. I often wonder how that might have changed my daughter's life. She is quite happy doing what she does today. She is a terrific wife and mother and has her Bachelor degree in Early Childhood Education. Her quiet personality wouldn't have suited the sometimes cut-throat demands of modelling. She still looks like a model today. I call her my 'real lady' daughter — so special and different in many ways from my other daughters.

*M*any people have told me my mother was known as the glamour girl of OPAL. She attempted to present herself in a dignified and commanding manner — full of confidence, self-assured in every respect, defying and being the ultimate exception to the Aboriginal stereotypes existing at the time. Muriel Langford often ironically said that 'Rita walked on the land as if she owned it'. She was a facilitator between two cultures which were like chalk and cheese — the oppressed and oppressor — but trod this difficult line with grace, ease and dignity.

Ah, OPAL, where would we kids have been without such a positive force in our lives? A force that kept the public self of Rita most respectable and exceptional for an Aboriginal woman of her time. It gave us another extended family on top of our own and provided a sanctuary for us. We were made to feel wanted and loved there, almost as if we were on public display. We got new clothes and shoes when we accompanied our mother on her talks. More importantly, we met other kids who know us now as thirty-something adults. It's great when we sit down and reminisce, laughing about the camps, socials, and the good old days.

OPAL provided a sense of belonging for us when we were children, supporting and extending our sense of kin. Among Aboriginals is a very strong sense of kin, of family and belonging. Like most Aboriginals, my family participate in a kinship system which extends well beyond the primary family of parents, siblings and children and secondary relatives to include great-aunts, great-uncles, second, third and fourth cousins, *great-nieces and great-nephews and more distant kin. Some of these relationships, especially those with seldom seen and spoken to distant kin, are complex and sometimes unclear to ourselves, and even more unclear to Europeans. Children participate with their parents in keeping in touch with kin, providing hospitality to them and sharing the family home with them. They learn early, by example, how to treat their kin, as well as becoming acquainted with a permanent and transient large kin pool. An extensive kin system works for a disadvantaged group as a strong resource in times of hardship.*

Not only have we, as Rita's children, learnt to value social relationships with our family, kin and community, but we are bound to them with pleasant memories. Our parental and sibling bonds remain strong, perhaps even stronger than the marital bonds established later. It is interesting to note that when others might turn from their parents, children and siblings, Aboriginal families, especially the mothers, daughters, sisters and nieces, do not. Other Australians might find the emotional expression of kinship bonds somewhat disconcerting, especially those which involve an extensive kinship system in the cities.

OPAL was a large and sometimes annoying part of our lives. We recall being constantly dragged around to dances, socials and talks on Aboriginal culture with our mother. Always displaying her very deep sense of pride in her Aboriginality, Mum was able to instill this in her children by speaking freely for hours in the halls of OPAL to other people about Aboriginals. She not only educated others but also educated us to respect our people and recognise we all had worthy contributions to make.

OPAL also allowed my mother and us to communicate with different groups of people from all walks of life, from politicians to business people, without feeling inferior. In those days people in the OPAL circles were keen to listen. This ability to comfortably interact and socialise with different people and not feel shame has carried through to today.

Not only did the OPAL experience equip us with social skills, but it provided a political framework from which to operate. For example, as a young teenager I became angry at the injustices dealt to Aboriginals and wished to pursue areas to overcome these injustices. However I realised that an aggressive stance could have created a reactionary response, alienating even the best intentioned people. Therefore I have attempted (and failed a few times) to concentrate on an accurate and sincere yet cogent oral and written style which not only interests people but urges them to reconsider their perceptions about Aboriginal people.

Such was the influence of OPAL, that as Rita's children we are determined that our children will be encouraged to explore and deal with the historical, political, social and cultural aspects of their Aboriginality through an activity or community involvement such as OPAL. OPAL affirmed a positive feeling that has made an enormous impact on our lives. Meeting Aboriginals and empathetic non-Aboriginals has provided lasting friendships, not only for my mother's generation but also for ours and our children's generations.

One of the most important things Aboriginal people can do for their children is to instil a dignified purpose and strong identity of being Aboriginal. This is the foundation for their future and costs nothing. It is a duty we all have to ourselves and our next generations. To be proud to say who we are and what we are without any feeling of inferiority is one of the greatest gifts of life we can give to our children. A secure identity base is the basic ingredient for the hazardous road ahead. This is what my mother has given to me and her children and grandchildren.

New forms of Aboriginal political organisation began in the '70s. Those years saw the beginning of an Aboriginal outspokenness that had never been witnessed before. Whereas in the '60s, OPAL had been one of only a few Aboriginal organisations, in 1972 with the Whitlam government in power there came increased funding and the establishment of Aboriginal and Torres Strait Islander organisations throughout the country. Some of these include Black housing, legal and health services. The late Pastor Don Brady was responsible for setting up the majority of these community-controlled organisations in Brisbane. They are evidence of our growing pride and sense of identity.

In cities and towns across Australia, these organisations are intrinsic to the fabric of Aboriginal society. They are places where Aboriginal people can meet without feeling inhibited or afraid. The organisations are predominantly staffed by Aboriginal people and so the services that are offered are culturally appropriate. For example, Aboriginal legal services will deal with issues that face Aboriginal people, such as incarceration, in radically different ways than a non-Aboriginal service. With the existence of these organisations, Aboriginal people have been relieved of some of the burdens that my mother's generation endured.

Aboriginal people have always wanted to take care of our own destinies. We don't want to be forever dependent on governments or the people who hold the purse strings. Yet government departments still seek to control our lives. Aboriginal people are then blamed for possessing a 'hand-out' mentality rather than being seen as victims of over 200 years of white exploitation. Everything that has happened for Aboriginal people in this country has been at the initiative of Aboriginal people themselves. If programmes are not Aboriginal-initiated, they are doomed to fail.

There has been some degree of goodwill on the part of non-Aboriginals but largely the achievements have come from the blood, sweat and tears of our people fighting for justice and equal rights. We are still frustrated in this endeavour, though, by the ingrained racism of non-Aboriginal Australia.

CHAPTER SEVEN

Coming Back to Earth

I N 1974, I'D BEEN AWAY, up north to Darwin and Bathurst Island, working on a project, based at the University of Queensland, researching Aboriginal education. It was a wonderful time, my first and only paid work outside domestic service. But I came back to a tragedy at home.

I'd rung my family to say when I was coming back, and ask if I could be met at the airport. The anticipation to see them all again mounted my body as I boarded the plane. I was completely unprepared for what was to happen.

When the plane landed I could not see my family anywhere. There to meet me was Dr Betty Watts from the University of Queensland whose research team I had been working with up north. I asked her to wait a while because my children would be there soon. Little did I know that a newsflash told of the disaster on televisions at the airport. I kept wondering where they were as Jackie was always so punctual. After an hour of waiting I gave up and Betty drove me home where Ngaire and Rodney were waiting for me. Twenty minutes later the phone rang — it was the police asking if I had arrived from Western Australia. Ngaire and Rodney met the police at the door a few minutes later. Immediately after, I heard Ngaire burst into tears. They told us that there had been a car accident on the way to the airport to pick me up and that Jackie had been killed and John had only a fifty/fifty chance of survival.

My whole body went completely numb for ages. I couldn't comprehend what they were telling me. This can't be happening to us, I kept thinking, it only happens to other people. I was in a haze when the police raced me up to the hospital, where I found my darling daughter Gloria had died and Mutoo, Jackie and John were in hospital. Mutoo was discharged later while Jackie spent two weeks in hospital. John would spend ten months and, following that, another long time to rehabilitate.

Gloria had four children — Jason, who was three years, Doods-Sherrin, five, Deeveena, six, and William John, who we called Kenny, was seven. When I told the children what had happened and that Mummy wasn't coming home anymore, we hugged each other and cried uncontrollably.

Gloria had been married at eighteen, and had had her children by her twenty-third birthday. My darling daughter seemed nearly always brunjabai in the first years of her marriage. Gloria had separated from her husband and so it was so natural for me to take on her children. They were the flesh and blood of someone I loved and still do so dearly. I could never have seen them go to a home. I've always had a fear of children's homes. To be taken away from your family is to me a fate worse than death. Not to know who your people are is tragic also. It's so important to keep the family together.

About a year after Gloria left us, Jason, her youngest, was playing in the garden and announced that when he died he wanted to be buried in the same hole as me. He must have been thinking of his darling mother at the time, remembering her funeral which must be so confusing to a small child, and perhaps worrying that I might die and leave him, too. You can never really know what grief children must feel at the loss of their mother when they are so very young. I'm sure that this has played a huge role in my grandchildren's lives.

At fifty-five, I became a mother again. The intense pressure and responsibility drove me womba at times. But Gloria's children were so special to me because I reared them. I had to make a big adjustment to my life, restricted my social life and stopped drinking. The children were more important to me, and I was afraid of losing them. I had to give them a decent home and stop the gypsy life that my children had led.

The children's aunties and uncle were too young to relate to them as mothers and fathers and it was unfair to put that on them. They were just beginning their lives. Ngaire married shortly after the accident. As the children grew up, the generation gap began to widen. This gap exists today and causes many conflicts at times between my grandchildren and me. We can go for weeks being sulky with one another. Then there is always something that brings us back together again. They know I love them even though we fight. It's as if this conflict is healthy and necessary

(Left to right) Jason, Sherrin, Deeveena and Kenny Murphy, 1981

105

to our lives. We have a saying that it's about time we all had a fight to keep us happy.

The accident had brought about huge changes in all our lives, not only mine and my grandchildren. My son Johnny was very seriously injured in the accident, and his recovery from the accident has been nothing short of a miracle. My family are all fighters but our greatest fighter is Johnny. Some physical signs of the accident are still there, but he still has the keenest sense of humour out of all my family. It is a credit to his determination and will to live and succeed. He is very modest about his achievements and I am so very proud of him. I spent many hours driving him to his rehab programmes and jobs. It seemed a struggle in those days but it all turned out for the best. It was worth it to see him getting stronger and improving every day. Johnny had been doing years of voluntary community work when he landed a good job in 1984 in Cairns, where he still remains today. He loves Cairns and doesn't look like leaving.

Out of his big generosity, Johnny used his accident insurance money to buy a larger house for my growing family near to the school. Without that secure home the task of caring for my grandchildren would have been even harder. Our new home had four bedrooms and so could house us quite well. We have lived here ever since and it's a real family home. I have a strong attachment to this place and hate to leave it because it's where my grandchildren grew up. My only sadness is that I have only seen Aboriginal families come and go from around here. And, come to think of it, this is why property valuations are up so high! In the early days my late brother Lawrence and his family lived not far from where we live now.

Nearby is the school where my grandchildren went, except for Kenny. Because Kenny's chronic asthma made him miss a lot of schooling he went to special schools. Montrose was a home for 'crippled' children as they called them then. This is where he spent his early years. His illness continued and later he went to Mitchellton Special School. He had a high intelligence, my Kenny.

One day I remember being invited to a meet-the-parents night at the children's primary school and thought I'd better go as I had shied away from them in the past. It was to be my first and last visit as nobody would speak to me and ignored me as if I was invisible. The only person who spoke to me was the tea-lady. It was like one of those 'Black is' (having the only vacant seat next to you on a peak-hour bus) jokes. This kind of rejection turned me off any further dealings with my grandchildren's education, whether it was primary or high school. And I had wondered how many other Aboriginal people had to go through the same experience. It's that feeling of being inferior and having nothing to contribute when it is the exact opposite. How much better the schooling system would be if it taught Aboriginal culture. My knowing about Aboriginal culture — storytelling, legends, song and dance — was not valued.

Although it hurts, I have always risen above it because to dwell on it only hurts you in the end. I certainly remember these things but never let them get to me like I've seen them get to other people. Some people will go on about it for days, weeks, months and years but it is only being painful to them. I try to do positive things to help me get over that pain. The lack of bitterness in Aboriginal people can be put down to the great humanness of our society. After what we've all been through, it's no wonder we are strong. I forgive sometimes and find it hard to forgive at other times.

The ones I've least forgiven are my own people because I expect much more from them, whether they are friends or relations, than I would from white people. When I've been hurt, it cuts like a knife and I like to give back as much as I can. My great achievement is having the final word and that's what makes me really happy — to hear my voice echo the last words. I see this in my son and grandson. My granddaughters make weak attempts whereas my daughters don't even try as they know I'm the champion at this game. They let me have my way. I have to win at something.

I've never been one to let things get me down too much. When the strain of raising a second family became too much I'd do what I've always liked to do — head for the bush. In 1976 I had an old, blue, EH Holden station wagon. It was a faithful old thing, so reliable and only needed fuel, water and oil. The time had come for me and the kids to have a holiday, so we packed it up to the hilt and drove north to Maryborough. Old Frank had spent much of his life in Maryborough and his wife and daughter were buried there. He used to knock around with many Aboriginal and Islander people in Hervey Bay. When I asked if he'd like to come with us he couldn't believe his good luck. He talked about it for weeks before we left and sat in the front seat all the way (much to the kids' disgust). As we passed certain places he'd talk about the things he did here and there. He must have had a full and interesting life, our old Frank. I heard he died some years back now. He was honest as the day he was born and seemed a very lonely old man and my heart went out to him because he had no family and friends.

We stayed in a caravan park at Hervey Bay and caught the ferry over to Fraser Island. While we were there, the movie *Eliza Fraser* was being shot. My hair wasn't as grey as it is now but if it had been I'm sure I would have been asked to play a starring role. I'd stop at showing my ngumuns, though. There were huge tents to accommodate the cast. It was fenced off from the day trippers and tourists. We were sitting on the beach when I spotted an older Aboriginal woman doing her washing in a small tub near the fence. I waved at her and she waved back. I went over and she looked pleased to see another Aboriginal person. She asked me where I was from and what I was doing there. After a little while she looked at me wearily and said, 'I'll be glad when we go back home. I'm not cut out to be a filum star'.

Not long after our tragedy, in September 1974, Ngaire married Rodney Jarro at Banyo Catholic Church. I am a great believer that every sadness gets replaced with a happy occasion and this was no exception. Over three hundred guests attended which included mostly relations, but I had become so carried away that I invited everyone I knew from the scout master, shopkeeper, to the people who had left their horses at our farm. Much to my surprise and without written invitations they came! No wonder Ngaire and Rodney had blank looks on their faces when some of the 'invited' guests congratulated them. It was a great day and I wanted to share it with the world.

Ngaire's wedding day, with her uncle, Oliver Holt, 1974

Despite the bridal party getting lost and being three-quarters of an hour late for the service, my brother Oliver was patient and so proud to give his niece away. His daughter Rhonda was one of the bridesmaids along with Jackie and cute flowergirl Deeveena who was given strict orders to keep her eyes straight ahead but instead kept looking around to see who was watching her. She hasn't changed much. (*Nah!*)

The bridesmaids' dresses were made in Ngaire's favourite colour, blue. I wore a blue dress (but made sure I didn't outdo them) with my hair up. Rodney's brother Moonchie was groomsman and his brother Brian was page boy. They looked nice in their suits as did the best man and Jackie's then-boyfriend who was widely known for his wacky sense of humour. He asked Jackie — who still had her jaw wired up in a brace from the accident — had she used brasso on her teeth that day to shine them up for the wedding. She nearly gave him a locked jaw then! I thought it was going to be on for young and old.

Uncle George held out Ngaire's veil and was crying in the church for his niece. Ngaire looked beautiful. I'd never seen my daughter looking so radiant. She floated down the aisle and told me later she felt so nervous but it didn't show at all. The day was made for her and my handsome son-in-law. Rodney had long hair and a mo to go with it. Both of them smiled and smiled all day. The weather was perfect and we were finally happy again after what we had just gone through.

My two old schoolmates from Cherbourg days, Carol Archer and Enid Bligh who are no longer with us, catered for the wedding reception which was held in the old OPAL Centre in Ann Street. They home-cooked everything. The meal was a smorgasbord of meats and salads, curry and rice, a variety of other hot and cold dishes and tasty puddings and sweets. No recipe books were needed here as, like me, my two friends were self-taught cooks. Us Aboriginal women sure can cook and make a dish go a long way, and did we ever need it that day.

Ngaire has inherited my domestic skills. She is a spotless housekeeper, wonderful cook and a doting mother to her three boys Rodney Jr, Nathan, and Bradley (BJ). I have a saying that when God gave her a husband he gave me a son. I love my son-in-law Rodney (we call him Rockie) as he's the best anyone could wish for. He had his own building business and worked seven days a week, usually twelve hours or more a day. The only days I've seen him take off were Father's Day, Mother's Day and his birthday. Today he works in the public service. He is building their own home, not far away from us, on weekends. So he's still working seven days a week.

Rodney grew up in Woorabinda and I call him the little boy who made good in the city. He had nothing and to see how he's worked so hard to achieve what he's got today is a miracle. They are such a tight-knit family. It is so nice to see families like that these days.

Ngaire Jarro with her husband and sons at the Holt family reunion, 1991. (Left to right) Nathan, Ngaire with Brad, Rodney Sr, Rodney Jr.

Ngaire is a real lady. She has always been a softie, so good and kind to people. She also has another side, like me, that only those close to her can see. I have a real temper when I'm stirred up and I tend to get easily upset these days. My tolerance used to be greater years ago. I've always believed that a good old argument never hurt anyone. In fact, my regular ones are good for me.

Ngaire's children are all good at sport, especially Bradley. That kid can run like a gazelle, jump like a grasshopper, and swim like a fish. He's always winning school events and one day I'm sure he'll represent Australia. Rodney Jr was a Queensland schoolboy rugby union rep. Nathan is the most academic of the three and wants to do economics, business and Japanese. He'll probably be Prime Minister someday.

All my grandchildren are interested in their culture. Rodney Jr has always been proud of his heritage from a very young age. When he was about seven we were watching a western on TV and he said proudly that he was on the Indian's side because the cowboys stole the land from the Indians in the first place. I thought how very smart that was. With comments like that I knew he would grow up to be a fine boy.

CHAPTER EIGHT

The Old Rugged Cross

G LORIA'S LEAVING US FOLLOWED the second major tragedy of my life after losing Jack and that was losing my mother in July 1973. My sister Thelma had rung me to say Mama was very low and slowly dying and to come up to Cherbourg. When I arrived at the hospital she asked, 'Rita, where Dadda?' A lump came to my throat and the tears fell. I asked her if she wanted some food, some guvung, and she said, 'Yes'. So I got a little tiny teaspoon but she didn't open her mouth so I never forced it down. Thelma took over to comfort her.

After a few days visiting her in hospital I went back to Brisbane to the children. When someone dies in our Aboriginal community, we believe we get a sign. There is a strong belief that the messages come through an animal or a bird. We call it the death bird. It was no different for me. I got up early one morning and I looked through our window. On our jacaranda tree in the backyard I saw a black crow, perched on a branch right at the top. His arms were outstretched and the rest of his body was straight. It was in the sign of a cross and suddenly his beak raised up and he looked right at me. I knew that Mama had left us then. Not long after, I got a phone call to say Mama had passed away.

When you lose your mother, you lose part of yourself.

Her funeral was so beautiful. They had put her in a coffin on top of an old dray led by a draught horse. The coffin was made by Aboriginal people who were so used to making things with their hands. They made their own houses, they made the cupboards and the chairs. Many of our men worked in the local sawmill and so there was plenty of wood around.

When we dressed Mama, her eyes were open. We don't like our dead people looking at us so we closed her eyes. We put flowers in her hair and she looked so peaceful. When I bent down to kiss her she was as cold as ice. We walked from the hospital to the gravesite behind the dray. Everyone was wailing and crying. 'Who's gonna be next?', the old people asked themselves. They had seen their people come and go.

The Christian ceremony began a few hours after the men had dug out and prepared Mama's grave alongside Dadda's. Gylma was going to be with him now. I was so overcome by grief that I hardly remember anything more except seeing her body being given back to the earth from where it came. We sprinkled a handful of dirt into the grave to show respect and let her spirit rest.

At the Cherbourg cemetery, there are hundreds and hundreds of crosses, painted white, to mark the graves. It looks so natural and the grass is growing on the graves. I feel as if the people are speaking to me when I sit down and listen to their voices in the wind.

After the ceremony, people came back to my mother's house. Hundreds came and went that day, one lot goes and another comes which is not unusual at Aboriginal funerals. We had cups of tea, damper and biscuits. It was a time to catch up with those relatives and old friends who we seldom see. We spoke about my adoring mother Gylma and what a gracious lady she was. People passed on their condolences and those of others who could not attend.

Cherbourg like many other Aboriginal communities has lots of dogs. When funerals are on, the dogs are fed to the hilt and never bark, remaining quiet all day and night. There are never any dog fights either. It's as if they behave themselves and pay their respects, too.

Mama's funeral was conducted by the Aborigines' Inland Mission (AIM). In the early days it was the only church on Cherbourg. The AIM was set up in 1905 by the missionaries who were sent to work all over Australia. When I was a girl at Cherbourg, Miss Shankleton, Mrs Long and Mr Brainwood were the missionaries that I had a lot of respect for. They seemed to love the Aboriginal people and valued our culture. They didn't stop us from speaking our language as others did. I would only accept advice from these missionaries and help them if I felt they were not taking my culture away from me.

Even though the missionaries had control, our spiritual life and white religion existed together somehow. It's a strange thing but we had a spirit in common. I hate people knocking religion because I believe there is something in it. There is a spirit inside everyone. It just chooses to come out or not. I don't know any Aboriginal people who don't believe in something.

During my OPAL days, religion remained. I tried to keep it separate from OPAL and it didn't worry my work there. I went to OPAL during the week and church on the weekends. The spiritual, working and peaceful life kept me going. I went to the Salvation Army church near us in Inala Avenue. One day I sent the kids to Sunday School and as I was walking past the bushes I heard this little voice say, 'Hi Mummy'. I looked and there were three pairs of black eyes looking through the grass. Then I heard a scuffle as they all came out blaming Johnny for calling out. He'd blown their cover.

Later, my good friend the late June Bond introduced me to the Inala Church of England. I'd take the kids as often as I could but again they wagged it. Instead of going to Sunday School they'd go off to the Bond's house in time for the ice-cream man. In the end, I gave up making them go.

I went to church by myself as a mother and grandmother because I felt I needed some spiritual help to cope with the responsibility of raising my children and grandchildren by myself. The thought was a burden at times. I did it, though, with the help of someone up there.

I have dabbled in different religions. These have been the usual Christian ones, Anglican, Uniting Church, Pentecostal and I've even tried Ba' Hai. There is a certain strength about them and it gives me great comfort to attend a church service when I have many fears and troubles. By sharing my problems with somebody, it takes the burdens away.

Although I don't attend services regularly these days, I am still a firm believer. The Church I came to feel most about is the Aboriginal Church at Paddington. The services are lively and soulful. We had services there which talked about Aboriginal culture, which is what I like. It also talked about real life things. The services are usually taken by an Aboriginal pastor who brings his family along. His extended family and friends come also. The attendance is usually small. The sermon is often about our families, communities and ways of life. Sometimes white people who are married to Aboriginal people or who know about Aboriginal culture come along, too.

Serious issues are talked about — death, poverty, alcoholism, violence, employment, gaol, involvement in the community, National Aboriginal Week and many more. And people from the congregation are invited to speak about any problems they might have. We are then asked if we can do anything to help those people less fortunate than we are. Perhaps it is the friendliness that is the most important thing about Aboriginal churches.

Strangers are taken into the congregation just like strangers are taken into the family, especially if they are Murries from out of town. We all have connections right across Australia so they are bound to be known to someone among us. We are able sometimes to put them in touch with their mob in Brisbane, too.

Journeying

MOSTLY WHEN I LEAVE my country and meet with
Aboriginal people from other places I feel a sense of
belonging, of being known. In 1974, I travelled to the
Northern Territory and Western Australia as part of a research
team, and wherever we went I felt welcomed by the Aboriginal
people.

I had been approached by Dr Betty Watts of the University
of Queensland to join her team which was investigating
Aboriginal education. As my children were then in their teens,
I jumped at the chance. It was the only paid job I would ever
do outside domestic service. We talked to students, parents,
teachers and principals in high schools about the sorts of issues
that affected Aboriginal students — Abstudy allowance, the
curriculum, teaching methods, Aboriginal schooling and white
schooling. My job was the link between the researcher and the
Aboriginal people.

*The education system has largely failed Aboriginal students but so
often the children are blamed and not the system.
White education has treated Aboriginal culture as if it is inferior to
European culture, and this takes away the Aboriginal children's pride
in their own culture. They are taught that the white way of doing things*

119

is the right way. Aboriginal people believe that today we need to prepare our children to keep their own sense of being Aboriginal people with our own culture as well as learning those things that will help them in the dominant Australian community.

We went to Bathurst Island and interviewed the Tiwi people. The island is a gorgeous place and I couldn't get over the number of Aboriginal people there. They were everywhere. We made several trips to Mowanjin, outside Derby. The people were friendly and I brought back carved and painted boab nuts, boomerangs, woomera and bags. We went to the Kimberleys where we were welcomed again. I will never get over how people trusted us. Like most Aboriginal people, they must get sick of talking, talking, talking, but they were so gracious in every reply, explaining what was wrong and how things could be improved. Always patient, answering our questions like it was the first time they'd been asked. But perhaps they were like me, talking in the hope that some day they will be heard.

Ever since that trip, the Kimberleys had been haunting me and I wanted to return there. They are so rich in culture. And then it happened that a trip was possible. In 1981, Reg and Margie Birch invited us to the Kimberleys, their country. For my grandchildren and for Jackie and me, it was a highlight of our lives.

Jackie had worked with Reg in 1978 in the National Aboriginal Conference (NAC) Secretariat in Canberra. He and Margie are Kimberley born and bred. They are so close to their culture, language and stories. All this will be passed down to their children and their children and their children so that the culture will never be lost. Reggie and Margie are like son and daughter to me. Their two sons, David and Simon, and two daughters, Robyn and Wendy, who are about the same ages as

Gloria's children, are like my own grandchildren. There is a strong link between us, as if we have all been family in another spiritual world. I think of them often and wish that we saw more of each other.

Reg is a tall, handsome, green-eyed, brown-skinned man. He has a deep voice and an even deeper commitment to helping his people. He became the NAC representative for his area in the Kimberleys in 1978, then worked as chairman of the Kimberley Land Council in Derby and was a commissioner with the Aboriginal and Torres Strait Islander Commission (ATSIC). When he and Jackie met, she told him she had a mother who would just adore him, and so I did. And then I met his lovely wife. Margie is a lovely lady who is every inch the woman in front of her man. She always kept the home fires burning and kept the family together while Reg had been away travelling. She has been the real power behind Reg's success as a spokesman. She has always been there for him.

The Kimberley mob are very friendly and hospitable and we soon made friends. What strikes me most about the Kimberleys is the number of Aboriginal people living there. They seemed to feel so comfortable. Maybe it's because there are so many of them and because they are on their own land.

We met Margie's cousin Joan Mader and her mother. We immediately hit it off as we had a lot in common like love of the outdoors, fishing, going to church, collecting bush tucker, hunting and family. Sadly, Joan's mother has passed away now. Joan's two boys, Stacey and Wayne, and my grandchildren would always come along on our local trips with us. We drove to Turkey Creek to see Joan's grandmother who must be well in her nineties by now and a lovely old girl. We arrived there with big boxes of groceries. While Grannie greeted her family with hugs and kisses, she was a little shy with the strangers at our first meeting. But she and I were soon comfortable with each other. Being an elder and speaker of her land, she is also a traditional owner.

121

Joan is an attractive woman with red hair and freckles and every inch an Aboriginal. When she goes to conferences, people look at her but are put straight as soon as she opens her mouth. She has represented the Kimberleys at many state-wide conferences on health, education, employment, church or law issues. She was Reg's NAC secretary and like the Birches she is a fighter for her people.

We went out-bush a lot, fishing, shooting and just driving. One day we came across a little creek where baby perch were fighting to jump onto our lines. They were so tiny, though, we just threw them back but it taught my 'city-ites' how to cast in fish. They've never had it so easy to this day.

We took some rounds of ammunition as well, in case we saw a kangaroo or other bush tucker. Reggie told Jackie to put the unspent bullets back in the magazine. Later, when he couldn't find them, he asked her where they were. She pulled out a *Woman's Day* and said, 'Here! D-o-n-t'. She didn't know what a gun magazine was. That's how cityfied my children are. Jackie didn't stay for long as she had to return to work. My grandchildren and I stayed for three months.

As with my children, my granchildren loved sport. Sherrin was a very fast runner and went in an event for the local school's sports day. She was up against some pretty fast Kimberley competition. One young girl was tipped to win outright but as they lined up I felt the excitement rise in my body. Bang! went the starter's gun. And they were off! The favourite led for most of the way. Then — zap! — Sherrin passed her and led all the way to the finishing line. There was a complete silence after the race and my family and I were the only ones left shouting and clapping.

Kenny's health improved. There is a picture I still have of Kenny wearing a hat with a rifle perched on his leg. The sleeves of his shirt were cut out and he looked like Wild Bill Cody. He loved the photo as it made him look so macho.

M *y nieces and nephews have told me that the time spent in the Kimberleys was some of the best days of their lives. They not only enjoyed the company of the many other children of their own ages but saw the diversity of Aboriginal culture and peoples at first hand. They were city kids who'd never been out bush before, and to witness how the Kimberley mob worked in with their land was an extraordinary thing for them. You can take so much for granted living in the cities.*

Being outside our own place can be difficult, though.

In 1988, after finishing her degree in history and anthropology at the University of Queensland, Jackie did a diploma in Aboriginal education at Flinders University in South Australia. As part of her course, she spent eight weeks teaching in Ti Tree, two hours drive north of Alice Springs, and John Henry (who likes to be called John these days) and I went with her. John was three years old then and I was glad to look after him while

Jackie and John (photograph by Angela Bailey)

123

Jackie was teaching. We were given a house across the road from the school. My grandson was so cute. Every morning, he would perch on the sink to wave his mum goodbye.

It was a good chance to meet the local Aboriginal people and learn their customs. They were Anmatjera people and I formed a wonderful friendship with the school's laundry lady, Nita Napparula. Nita was a tall, strong woman. Her hair was curly and reminded me more of the Torres Strait Islander people.

Being 'outsiders' and new in town some Adelaide friends called in on their way from Katherine. They asked about us at the service station. The local, white, school bus driver was having his tea in the diner. Our friends went over to him to find out where they could find us. He replied that he knew of an Islander family who were living in the town, and swore black and blue that we weren't Aboriginal (good-go). This was because we spoke a different language and my hair was frizzy. Usually my hair is thin and straight but I'd recently had a perm which had sent it crazy.

It was then that I realised how different we were, not only to the whites in town, but to the Aboriginal people. I am sure they saw Jackie as a white person because she was a teacher and couldn't speak her own language apart from the Aboriginal English we use between ourselves. For the first time in Jackie's life she suffered from an identity crisis — she was too black to be white and too white to be Black. And I am not sure they knew what to think of me. Here I was, this little old granny looking after a small boy but still very different from them. They were very wary of us but I was determined to be myself and break down the barriers. Acceptance took some time, but it did come. After school and in the early evening the children and their families would come around and it was not unusual to have twenty people in the house. Acceptance came more quickly for me, though, than it did for Jackie as she was seen as a boss figure. The kids called her 'Miss Jackie' at school and at home.

I have always been strong about my Blackness. From my earliest days my mother, family and friends helped me to feel pride in being Black, and I've been reminded of my difference by whites ever since. Without that early reinforcement I'd be a confused person now. Until Ti Tree I had never questioned where I stood in the world. I was a person within a white world. But in Ti Tree I was a Black person within a Black world that was different from my own and I experienced something of a culture shock.

But all the same, here the white world still wielded the power.

My uneasiness was apparent to the young Black children that I taught and their families. The children were my greatest critics. We all weren't sure what to make of each other. They were privileged in their own way but I felt as though I had a privilege that exceeded theirs but could never exceed the white privilege. But what is privilege anyhow and who really holds it? They probably pitied me the most.

Jackie would come home and tell us how her day was with the children. She did not approve of the white teaching but loved the children. They weren't cheeky and gave her a lot of satisfaction.

One day she asked a class of five white children and twenty Aboriginal children whose families had been living the longest in the area. A young white girl put her hand up and claimed that her grandparents had been living in the area for over fifty years. Jackie turned to a young Aboriginal boy and asked him how long his people had been there. 'I don't know, Miss, maybe thousands of years, ey?' 'Try 50,000, Sean', she said. With that, the Aboriginal pupils' pupils lit up like brown beacons across the room. She saw their proudness. They sat up quickly and had huge white smiles all over their mitha mitha faces. It seemed the white children were always in competition with the Aboriginal children. That is except when it came to sport. The Aboriginal kids always won. The white kids didn't like it either. For once in their lives the Aboriginal children had them beaten.

125

The days were beautiful and clear. I love the desert, so arid and majestic. At night we would sit outside in the glorious sunset. I would think about the old people who lived in the area long before I had ever seen this country. How contented they must have been.

During a long weekend we hired a car and went to Uluru, a place I had only dreamed about. I was overcome by its presence and beauty. A kindred spirit had opened up inside me. For one of the very few times in my life I was speechless as we drove around it. I noticed every little crevice and wondered how all the old people once survived in harmony around it. We drove into the Aboriginal township but it was deserted. We found out later all were at the Barunga Festival in Katherine.

When we were camping, I met a young English tourist, and I invited her to the Olgas with us the next day. Jackie was a bit cheesed off because I was always inviting strangers along. As we drove past Uluru, I pointed out the Aboriginal warrior's face on the rock. The English lass swore she could not see it. I've always wondered if it is only something Black people can see, as every Murrie I have spoken to who has been to Uluru has seen it.

To me there seems more of a spiritual presence at the Olgas than Uluru. Perhaps this is so because there appeared little European tampering here, and less goings-on by tourists. They'd climb the Rock out of an effort just to say they climbed it. I wonder if they thought about its sacredness, though. How typical, I think, of white people who are satisfied with the result rather than the purpose. My daughter refused to climb on her 'Mother's heart', as she described it. That trip was so brief but I'll never forget that beautiful place.

Sometimes white people don't think we have a right to be there. Or they have expectations that all Aboriginal people will be the same. Like the time Jackie and I went over to New Zealand for a holiday. It was an eye-opener for me. I saw another beautiful country and lots of sheep. This was a strange feeling to leave my country. I was a little frightened but had my big backstop with me. I'd never been out of Australia before.

When we arrived in Christchurch we went straight to our motel room and in the morning met up with people who were on our coach tour. We were a very mixed bunch of people — Americans, Australians, Canadians, Japanese and Europeans. I spotted a big, tall, Yankie tourist staring at us and said to Jackie, as I so often do, 'Thilly-wujaburri!' ('Big, white eyes watching us'.) He asked us 'what' we were and when I said we were Aboriginal he shook his head in disbelief and said he'd just been to Australia and, no, we weren't. Fancy saying that! I was very angry and told him that we knew who we were. I knew I had jarred him by the look on his face.

A Scottish lady, Ella, shyly came over and said, 'Excuse me, dear, are you...are you...the Aborigines?' Now we were the exotics. When I said, 'Yes', she took me over to meet her husband. They were nice people, and the four of us became good friends. We dined with each other every night. One night we were enjoying ourselves so much that I stayed up till the wee (pardon the pun) hours of the morning drinking. What I didn't know was that it was straight Scotch on the rocks I was drinking. Jackie retired to bed much earlier (as she couldn't handle the pace). I can still see her peering down the hall to see if I wouldn't fall over. It's strange that I never felt slightly tipsy although I must have drunk many, many glasses. I remember matching them drink for drink, but it had no effect on me. My sleep that night was rock solid. In fact, the next morning the bus driver said he had heard snores from our room. I'm not sure if that had been me or Jackie.

It was so interesting seeing a different land. My only regret is that we never met any Maori people.

*O*ur experience in New Zealand showed the preconceived ideas people have about Aboriginals. Because we did not fit the stereotype of the 'savage' we were not considered 'real' Aboriginals. You meet this often. Like the time it was said to me that I didn't sound like an Aboriginal because I didn't have an accent. Styles of dress, speech, abode, where we shop or what car we drive do not lessen our relation to Aboriginal culture and identity. Nor do they heal the emotional scars from our experiences living in western society.

The ultimate insult is 'You're not a real Aboriginal'. Non-Aboriginal people are not expected to comply to one particular model and neither should we. We come in all shapes and sizes, and from different places. We have always had to conform to white Australian society, but imagine what a different country Australia would be now if non-Aboriginals had had to adopt Aboriginal ways. Non-Aboriginals have a lot to learn from Aboriginals, things like respect for one another, cooperation rather than competition, non-materialism, looking after the country, taking care of family and respect for elders.

On our way back from New Zealand, we stopped over in Canberra for a week, but I was feeling very restless and disturbed about something. Jackie felt restless too but neither of us could put a finger on what it was. We'd just had a lovely time and shouldn't be worried about anything.

Ngaire and Rod had been minding the children for me while I was in New Zealand. Kenny was wheezing, which was usual, but his asthma seemed a lot worse. He greeted me warmly and was overjoyed to have his Nan home again. He made us cups of tea. He'd always enjoyed cooking and I felt one day he'd love to be a chef. Kenny was only eighteen but had a maturity far beyond that.

Rodney Sr was down that day and he and Kenny were doing some work and went downstairs. Suddenly Rod sang out to me to call the ambulance. As I rushed downstairs my heart sank. There was Kenny lying on the cement floor. We called Fred, our next-door-neighbour, who gave Kenny mouth-to-mouth resuscitation. I'll never forget Fred for that. He and his wife Betty are such wonderful neighbours. But Fred's efforts were all in vain. Sadly, Kenny passed away in my arms.

The tragedy of losing someone close to you is devastating. I had thought my world had fallen on me when I lost my Jack, mother and Gloria. But to have loved and lost my beautiful young grandson, the most good-natured of any of my family, that was the most heartbreaking thing to happen. 'Why so young?' I kept asking myself.

All those who knew Kenny were heartbroken. He was such a wonderful fellow. He'd laugh and join in; that is, of course, if his sickness allowed him. He loved life even though life did not love him. He fought almost daily to overcome his breathlessness. For weeks he could go on without an attack, the wheeze would always be there though. Then would come a huge attack which would hospitalise him for weeks on end. He had always been in and out of hospital. His short life was a constant battle but when he was well he'd be well. He loved us all so dearly and wanted to be big brother, protector, wiseman, comforter — all rolled into one. Ken was such a sensitive fellow who loved kids, especially babies. He was such a doter around them that he won his school medal for Mothercraft. I often think how great he would have been to our babies who came along after his passing, especially his nephews and nieces.

He never complained about his sickness when in fact he had so much to complain about. It hurt him to see us in pain over him. No matter how sick he was, he always looked on the bright side of life. He loved every well moment, the pleasure would be written all over his face. Trying to lead as normal a life as possible, he took up working at Coles, pushing trolleys. His workmates were really good to him there. He won them over with his charm, sincerity and warmth. He was truly one of life's treasures and we all miss my Kenny dearly.

Kenny had an infectious love about him. He oozed with warmth and vitality. His keen sense of humour would rub off on everybody. He'd make us laugh over nothing. There was also a special naive quality about my grandson. When he was entering his prime of life, just like his mother, he was taken from us. They say only the good die young and certainly the very good did in my family.

CHAPTER TEN

Barambah Gone Now

T HINGS ARE DIFFERENT in Cherbourg compared to how they used to be. Of course, everything changes with time. Sometimes change is for the best but I'm not sure if this is so for Cherbourg. It's Cherbourg now and will never be Barambah again, the place I grew up in. The old people and our happy times are gone now.

I see a big change in the lives of people at Cherbourg. We had no drinking, no drugs, no breaking up people's marriages. There's a lot of fighting and drinking going on now. You hear stories. We never had that because grog wasn't allowed then. (Sly grog got snuck in, though. Whiteman used to sell them grog.)

I never knew too much violence. People used to hit each other but then make up. They were very forgiving. But now I hear the violence is increasing. It breaks my heart to see what it's like today. It's hard for me to pass too much judgement because I don't want to condemn my people. I don't live in Cherbourg anymore and so what I hear comes through other people. All the gossip is over the phone. Sometimes people exaggerate but sometimes it's true. I don't like to speak ill of it too much.

In the past, there were more humpies and less whiteman's houses. The houses there today are modern and the new ones like white people's homes. There's an old saying, 'You can take

131

the Blackfella out of the mission but you can't take the mission out of the Blackfella'. That's so true. Our custom of sharing will never die out as long as we have relations. The bigger the house, the bigger the families who live there. There are some beautiful homes just recently built near the hospital. It's more a whiteman's way of living now. It's the same everywhere else in Australia.

For years the government ignored Cherbourg but when the Commonwealth Games came to Brisbane improvements were made to the homes. I believe a lot of money was spent then. The tourists wanted to visit an Aboriginal 'reservation' and Cherbourg was the nearest to the city. Years ago, we never had any visitors. They never used to want to know about Aboriginal people. But now they're very inquisitive about what makes a Blackfella tick and they want to go and visit us.

The corroboree and culture are things that will keep the place alive now. My two great grandsons dance in the corroboree group there. I was so proud to see them recently dancing at their parents' wedding. The people in Cherbourg are getting a better education now than we did because they put them through high school in Murgon. And the Aboriginal people who can afford it live in Murgon now.

They've got a beautiful emu farm on Cherbourg. It's a tourist attraction, you know. People come from all around to see it. They can eat the emu and get the eggs. Now they're selling the carved emu eggs not only in Cherbourg but all over Australia. They are so gifted. The fellas that make them I mean, not the emus.

But people are there and will always stay there. Like my sister Thelly. She has never moved away from the place. She told me that they wanted to put her in an old people's home but she refused to go. She said, 'No. My husband built this house. Every nail, timber and wood was done by him. I can't leave this place, see.' Her late husband Bumper Hegarty was a carpenter and builder. Her house is spotless, just like Mama taught us.

You hardly heard of domestic violence in my time and that's true. I never ever saw my father hit my mother. He wasn't a vicious man. I think that old yarraman got more hits than we did. He never hit the dog because the dog was too fast for him.

But now! Most Aboriginal families would know about it from their own experience. Mine is no exception. We've had it very close. Two of my granddaughters are going through it right this minute. It happens everywhere. No family would not be touched by it. Aboriginal people are not the only ones this happens to. It's a sign that something has gone wrong. No one likes to talk about it that much, although things are changing and it's becoming more in the open now. There are services available where you can go to speak to people about it. But, sadly, if we talk about it, it can be used against us, too. Usually we talk a lot about it together as family or friends.

My cousin Cissie West's family has suffered through violence. Cissie was my favourite cousin who I grew up with.

Cissie West with a grandson, Cherbourg

133

She married policeman Natie West and lived all her life at Cherbourg. They had a large family who she raised by herself after Natie died. Then she raised her grandchildren as well, like so many Cherbourg Aboriginal women have. She raised children all her life and felt a failure when her children and grandchildren would get in trouble with the law. She would pick them up from the Cherbourg dormitory or the police station on petty charges like being cheeky, drinking or swearing.

She was a kind soul and needed to get a rest. I would try to bring her down to Brisbane for a break, away from her family. When she came down, she'd always bring one of her grandchildren with her. It was usually Jeffo whose beautiful white smile would light up his ebony face. He had a lovely personality like most of her children and grandchildren, especially her daughter Tootie. Tootie looked like her mum and they call her

Tootie West
and
Laurence Holt

Queen of Musgrave Park,[1] and she is so regal the way she gives orders. The Park mob jump, too.

I remember going on a bus trip back to Cherbourg just before my cousin passed away. At the time she was having a few arguments with the administration there about the toilets. They were always out the back, and she wanted them inside. Cissie was getting older and the winters in Cherbourg are yukal. In the old homes the ceilings aren't even joined. She found it awful on nights to go outside to the toilets. In an argument with a councillor she said, 'All right, I'll fix you. I've got a niece who works in Canberra'. She told me about it some months later and by coincidence the toilets were now appearing in the houses. Cissie was delighted because she thought somehow Jackie had moved mountains in Canberra. She never forgot her niece for that.

Her funeral a few years later was one of the biggest in Cherbourg. She remained a strong Christian until her last days and worshipped every Sunday at the AIM. I love all her children and grandchildren and they always ring me up. In a way, I have taken the place of my dear cousin to them. They know they can come to me anytime. Her life was filled with sadness and many tragedies in her family. I'll never forget my darling cousin.

We've just been to the funeral of young Natasha, Cissie's granddaughter. Natasha was only twenty-four. So sad. We think she was murdered.

On the day of Natasha's funeral there were four other funerals at Cherbourg. Our people are still dying fast, and young. It was so hot and even hotter in the church where most of the people were sitting, waiting for the coffin to be brought in. I couldn't help thinking how many times I'd been in that church to see all the people I knew being buried. I could feel the spirits around me. The white pastor said it would be half an hour until the car with the coffin arrived. When Tootie heard that she was so frustrated and angry. She took off her shoes and banged them together overhead and threw them on the floor. She left the church, wailing and crying out. I wanted to go to her, but there were too many people to try to pass. Not long after that, the coffin arrived and Tootie came back in again. Everything was so quiet when they brought the coffin in.

Most Aboriginal funerals have an open coffin. I didn't have the strength to look. I wanted to remember Natasha just as I had last seen her — a beautiful young woman in Musgrave Park. As we sat in the church, I thought about Cissie, my favourite cousin, resting in peace now, not having to worry about her family anymore.

The service was a usual one, although our favourite Aboriginal hymn, The Old Rugged Cross, was sung. The white pastor was like other pastors; he didn't know much about our culture. The service wasn't personal and didn't say anything about Aboriginal people although most of us in the church were Aboriginal. It was like we weren't even there. I wasn't the only one feeling like that because a friend said when she goes she wants a traditional funeral.

My mind went back to how the old people must have performed the funerals in Carnarvon Gorge. They would wrap the bodies up in bark and leaves and put them in caves. The little babies would go on the branches of trees so the animals wouldn't get to them. I thought how clever my people were.

Today we have pieces left of traditional funerals. The service is done by an Aboriginal pastor who usually has had some Christian training. Sometimes there is a smoking ceremony. Leaves and bushes are burnt to cleanse the spirit. Smoke is collected in the cups of the hands and placed on the people, or people walk through the smoke to cleanse themselves of all evil spirits. It is such a powerful feeling when you go through smoking. The coffin sometimes gets smoked before it is put in the ground. Different tribes have different reasons and ways of doing the smoking. Sometimes men do it and sometimes women. I prefer that it's men's business.

Dances and songs in language are always done for traditional funerals. The boys and men paint themselves up and sing the songs beautifully. I see women's dancing coming back, too. Some young women dance with their brothers at funerals. Nearly everyone wears our red, black and yellow colours at traditional funerals. Our colours are simple and symbolic, and stand for black, the colour of our skin, yellow for the rising sun and the hope of better tomorrows and the future, red is for the earth and the blood that has been shed. The colours are well known today. I'm sure some white people think they're radical to wear, but we wear them with pride.

One day, I was at The Gap bank and a man spotted my watch. It has the Aboriginal colours on it. He said, 'I like your watch. It's a brand new day for your people, isn't it?' Well, it lifted my spirits up, to tell the truth. I just thought he was a businessman who wouldn't know or care anyway. It goes to show there are some people who do care. I treasure such moments because they don't come too often.

When there are sad times, happiness usually follows. Not long after Natasha's funeral, I went to Cherbourg for the wedding of my grandson Bally. Jason came up from Canberra to be best man for him. There must have been about three hundred people at the wedding. We had a lovely time.

I love going to Cherbourg for happy times, not sad. I have a different feeling, so free. When it's sad, it's like I'm trapped there still in my heart. I think about my parents a lot, the times we had, and always visit their graves. If only they could come back for a short time and see their children, grandchildren and great grandchildren. They'd be so happy. They were such wonderful parents. When I see Cherbourg I feel that they are still there, watching us come and go. No matter where I go, I will never stop going to Cherbourg. It was home to us for all those years. Not that we had a choice, of course. It was where our family was. We would have been all right anywhere as long as we had one another.

(1) Musgrave Park is in South Brisbane near the old Expo site and is a common meeting place for Murries. Even Expo came and went but the diehard Murries stayed. Expatriate Cherbourgites seem to have claimed it these days but there are Aboriginal people from all over the state who lob in looking for relatives and directions to other places. It is a place where Murries feel comfortable about having and sharing a drink and there is such a place in every town — Victoria Square in Adelaide, the Todd River in Alice Springs, under the bridge in Townsville, Charcoal Lane in Melbourne, just to name a few.

ELEVEN

Brand New Day

I N RECENT YEARS, ABORIGINAL people have been finding different ways to get our people's message across, and the arts have been one of the ways I like best. My favourite was the Aboriginal musical *Bran Nue Dae*. I went to see it five times because I thought it was the deadliest musical I had ever seen. It made me even prouder to be an Aboriginal, if that's possible. The young actors showed that there's plenty of natural talent around. Aboriginal people are born actors — we've had to act for most of our lives.

For those of you who didn't see it, one of the stars was Ernie Dingo. By sheer luck, a friend was in town who happened to know Ernie. He was kind enough to arrange a meeting with me and some members of my family. My grandson Nathan couldn't believe his eyes when the tall, dark, and handsome actor arrived. He glided in and shook hands with all of us. Then he naturally began telling stories and jokes. Everything that man says is funny but he can be so serious at the same time to get his point across to migaloos. He told us of a time he was performing in Perth. His opening line was: 'You know, all you whitefellas, I must be the only Blackfella in Australia that you actually pay to get up and abuse you all night'. I felt so happy to share half an hour of this man's busy life. He was charming and very down-to-earth. When I asked him if he was rich now, he replied, 'Hell, no. You know how it is, Mum. I got too many relations for that!' I knew what he meant.

Another star of the show was Stephen (Baamba) Albert from Broome. Could that man sing and play the guitar! We spent time with him and others who could meet us after the show.

On the final night I gathered all the 'old girls' down to the front row to watch. Having seen it so many times, I felt I now owned shares in the theatre and boldly asked the usherette if my friends and I could sit as close as possible. May McBride, Muriel Langford, Jessie Budby and Heather Tilberoo joined me. During the encore, some of the cast came down and grabbed us, and took us up on stage. All us girls were up there jiving and bopping away to the band Kuckles. Everyone was clapping. It felt so deadly to be there. We went backstage and then over to their farewell party. Quite a few people were there, singing and laughing away.

*A*ctually, I'm a bit of an actor myself. The great event was the play Is This Seat Taken? at the Space Theatre in Adelaide. I had latent actress tendencies at that time. I'm cured now.

The play was an interesting project. There were thirty Aboriginal women and thirty non-Aboriginal women. My only condition for taking part was to be allowed to sing Cherbourg Girl, *a condition that was accepted by the organisers. Little did they know I couldn't sing a note in key to save myself. Still can't. But as it turned out, my singing was well covered by the fabulous all-female band.*

The show was a cabaret about women's lives, taking on everything — child-rearing, land rights, and other political issues — with unending satire and humour. These experiences were presented in song, dance and sketches. The show confronted the stark contrasts and striking similarities in the lives of women from different cultures. The women in the play also learnt a lot about each other and have a lasting admiration and friendship for and with each other. It was a thrill to be involved in the warm and wonderful, sad and funny evenings of theatre.

My son looked splendid, specially dressed in a white suit and red bow tie to see his mum perform. He couldn't get over seeing me on the huge stage. When I came home late one night after a show, he jumped into his Gran's bed and told her, 'Mummy is a beer head again'. I didn't think he noticed.

Along with theatre productions, Aboriginal festivals have become strong in the past few years. On the Queen's Birthday weekend in 1989, I visited the annual Aboriginal festival at Barunga, just outside Katherine. The festival is a great celebration, and Aboriginals and non-Aboriginals come from all over the place to attend. I caught a bus from Darwin to Katherine to attend this great event. While in Katherine I met up with some local Aboriginal people who were also heading out to Barunga and offered me a lift.

Barunga has a carnival atmosphere with dancing, spear throwing and other cultural events. Hugh fires are lit up at nights so that people can sit around and talk. It is an alcohol-free event which I believe is a good thing. The festival gives people a chance to catch up with each other after a long absence. The football carnival is the most popular event of the festival. It was there that I spotted Nita from Ti Tree in the crowd and we were so happy to see each other that we hugged until our arms got sore. She was happy, too, because Ti Tree Football team had won the competition that day.

One of my favourite festivals has been the Maleny Folk Festival. Maleny is an hour's drive north of Brisbane on the

Boys from Cherbourg and Kuranda in North Queensland at the Maleny Folk Festival

Sunshine Coast. It's a beautiful spot, so lush and green. My friends, though, say that the Maleny Festival is becoming too popular. Certainly, a lot of people come. About 40,000 people attend each year and although it usually rains, it doesn't dampen our spirits. People camp out in the rain.

The festival has people from many countries participating to bring out awareness of their cultures. The festival is about love, hope, peace, joy, and a better future. I think it has the best Aboriginal acts of any other folk festival in the country: Archie Roach and Ruby Hunter, Joe Geia, The Mills Sisters, and the Tiddas. A few years ago, a highlight of the festival was the three Aboriginal dance groups who came together to perform corroboree for the first time in Maleny for over one hundred years. The Brisbane group Imbala hosted the event in which Milmarjah Dreaming and Djabugay Mona Mona Dancers from Kuranda performed. Fire was started in the traditional way. Boys as young

as five showed their skill, spindly legs shaking in the glow of the campfire. My heart filled with pride when I saw these dances. It will stay in my memory for a long time.

Jackie, Linda McBride-Levi and, star of stage and screen, singer Kevin Carmody, did a segment on Murrie humour and, although I'd heard some of the jokes many times before, they made me laugh again. Most Murrie humour and jokes come from events in our lives.

There was the story Jackie told of a Mexican colleague who visited a remote Aboriginal community at Ernabella, Central Australia. In the middle of winter, sitting cross-legged in the dirt near a fire, were two old Aboriginal men, rugged up in holey blankets, smoking dumpers and speaking language. She pulled up her Volkswagen, got out and went over to introduce herself. She could feel two sets of red eyes peering out at her from under grey, stained, felt hats.

'Hello', she said, 'Do you speak English?' After a minute or two of silence came, 'Yes', from the one sitting farthest away. The other man's shyness showed as he never said a word the whole time.

After some talk about the weather and why she was there, the friendly old man who had been inquisitively studying her long, thick, black hair and olive complexion said, 'Where you from, girl?
'Mexico', she replied.
'Oh...Mexico', he said, knowingly.
'Yes! Do you know where that is?' she asked in great surprise.
'Sure. I seen a video of it last week'. With that, he looked sadly at her and softly touched her on the arm: 'You p-o-o-r things!'

That shows the great regard we have for our fellow human beings because we think there has to be someone worse off than we are.

Linda and Kevin are two of the world's funniest raconteurs who can spin joke after joke. Their jokes are something like humorous chapters from *War and Peace* because they are so long. But they can hold an audience's attention right until the punch line.

Linda told the story of her lovely two-year-old daughter Georgia. Georgia is quite dark skinned, which she inherited from her dad James who is Afro-American, and Linda who isn't the fairest of lilies either. Georgia has a kinky-haired, black as the ace of spades, nugget shoe-polished doll called Gundu that Georgia takes with her everywhere. One day, Linda was pushing Georgia in a pram with Gundu who was dressed in the same pink coloured dress that Georgia was wearing that day. Linda could see a woman walking towards her smiling. As the woman got closer, Linda could see a funny look appearing across the woman's face. When they met the woman said, 'Oh, my gosh! I thought those two were twins!' This goes to show what whitefellas think that we all look alike.

Kevin told a joke about a stallion which is unrepeatable because my grandchildren will be reading this. However, there were other jokes.

Q: What's the difference between a computer and a Blackfella?
A: You only have to punch the computer once.

Q: What's the definition of an Aboriginal nuclear family?
A: Mum, Dad, the two kids and the anthropologist.

Another true story. A young Aboriginal mother turned to her whingeing five-year-old perched in a supermarket trolley and shouted: 'Ahh, wadda ya want?'
'Land rights!' came the loud reply.

Then a session called Twentieth-Century Dreaming was held under the Big Top, a huge circus tent. It was the largest venue of the festival and many people attended. It was a modern-day dreaming about what we wanted and expected for the future.

This event is the most popular every year and is heard by hundreds. Eight of us from all different ages, places and experiences spoke. When it came to my turn, I became overwhelmed with emotions because everything in life that I preached (although difficult at times) like love, caring and sharing came flooding into my mind. I told the audience that I hoped for an open peaceful society where we could all get along. It felt good to speak to people who shared these ideals. It was good, too, to hear people from other backgrounds than my own speaking about their lives and their efforts to hold onto their traditions in white Australia.

At the end, we danced and sang our farewells, and from now on I'll be a regular at the Maleny Folk Festival.

There are new kinds of meetings taking place among Aboriginal people now. There are many conferences, and they are for me now something like OPAL was for me in the '60s. These conferences are now my OPALs. They talk about the issues facing Aboriginal people in the '90s, like housing, the arts, justice, employment and domestic violence.

A very important event was the First International Indigenous Women's Conference, the dream of Jo Willmot. I call Jo our Guna Gully girl because she was born in Cherbourg, although she's lived in Adelaide for over twenty years now. Jo is such an articulate young Aboriginal woman, a determined organiser with a charismatic nature. She had a vision of indigenous women from all over the world coming together to speak of our concerns. She got the conference going without any funding — just a dream that it needed to happen and would. In July 1989 she and her committee succeeded in organising one of the greatest events for indigenous women around the world.

Three hundred participants had registered one week before. Fifteen hundred came. They came from everywhere. Women from all over the world joined to celebrate their cultures and to discuss future international networks for indigenous women. The opening of the conference was marked by a street march. Before women's business proper began there was a two-day ceremony, with dances, songs, poetry readings.

I met many of my own people there. But little did I know there were some white-skinned indigenous people. I thought we were all Black. They were the Sami people of Samiland. Other people call it Lapland but the Sami people don't use that word. I have often thought it would be nice, too, to have our indigenous name for Australia.

It was good to know that we aren't the only ones who have problems. There are people all over the world suffering. When you struggle daily and when survival is constantly on your mind, it's hard to see what else is happening around the world.

I was so taken by this conference that I went to the Second International Indigenous Women's Conference in Norway. I had saved some money that I could use towards my fares, but I didn't have enough. I really wanted to go and asked Jackie how she was holding. Little did I know she and the family were scheming to send me anyhow. So, with the bungu the family lent me, I went as an observer to the conference, held in Karasjok, and also onto Tromso where the World Conference of Indigenous Peoples was meeting.

Many topics were discussed, like mining and logging and nuclear weapons. I don't feel as educated and as political as the younger women, but all the same I hope that I made my contribution. When I came home, people said I was glowing, looking fitter and younger — which way. I certainly felt good. These events, like the Aboriginal community events in my own country, fill me with enormous energy and hope.

But it wasn't only a hopeful future that seemed real; the past came back to me too. I wanted to find my old friend Harry

Hapameni, who was living in Finland somewhere. I wasn't quite 'finnished' yet. I met four Swedes who took me over the Finnish border. Finnish networks are as amazing as ours. All I could tell them was his name — no address — just that he was a sailor. Within twenty-four hours they'd tracked him down. Sadly, he was at sea. I spoke to him on the phone: 'Do you remember a friend from Australia?' 'Hello, Rita! What are you doing in Finland?' I told him why I was over in his part of the world. He was so far out in the ocean that it would have taken him a week to get back. We promised to keep in touch. I haven't yet, but I will send him a copy of this book.

L ately in our conferences there has been revival of the spiritual aspect which complements the business proper. Our women's conferences especially are becoming times of good healing. Usually, the elders open the conferences which leaves a calming influence throughout the proceedings. In some cases, a healing ceremony is performed. This can take the form of smoking, dance, song, speaking or relaxation. There is an openness among us now for speaking about things in meetings like these.

The nature of our concerns as Aboriginal people is at times fiercely urgent and emotional, to the point that we can deal with them in no other time except the present So, in order to get our voices heard, we sometimes have to take drastic steps, such as stating the issues clearly in spite of who might hear them and whether it will offend them or not. There will be many more conferences to go to and as I write this, one is about to begin and a few more are being planned. Aboriginal affairs are a never-ending story with many chapters being written all the time.

One of the most recent conferences I've been to was the First National Aboriginal and Torres Strait Islander Women Writers Conference. Like Jackie says, the elders opened the conference. I spoke on the elders' panel to welcome everyone. Auntie Ida West from Tasmania was there and I really enjoyed meeting her. She speaks from the heart, that old woman.

People tell stories about their lives and what's happened to them, the things they've seen. Everybody likes listening to stories. Some stories are very strong and exciting; there are sad and happy stories. I like the sad stories coming out because it helps people. It gives Aboriginal people confidence to speak about our lives and to be listened to. I think it's good that Aboriginal people are writing down these stories. We've got a lot of things to say to the migaloos. They don't understand it all, of course.

At the conference we launched the Pitjaranda Trust for Aboriginal women writers and for other writers interested in Aboriginal history and culture. The Governor came and a few other big wigs, including government ministers. It was a good night.

CHAPTER TWELVE

The Gathering of the Clan

OUR HOLT FAMILY REUNION at the OPAL centre in Ann Street, Brisbane, came the night after the annual OPAL Ball in 1991 and so it was a huge weekend for us and our caterers, the Watego family, who did a beautiful job. My niece Brenda and my daughter Mutoo organised it lovely.

Our reunion was the first time we had been together as a family in our lives. A huge banner in Aboriginal colours said, 'Welcome To The Holt Family Reunion'. The beautiful cake had the bold letters HOLT on it. My brothers and sisters cut the cake.

It was an emotional time for all of us. We celebrated with our children, grandchildren, nieces and nephews. Mutoo presented us with gifts. The eldest child in each family gave gifts to their parents. A family tree was also made up. About one hundred adults and fifty children attended. My grandson Bally's band, Muddy Flats from Cherbourg, played songs I hadn't heard for years and good old country and western songs. Everyone was soon jiving away on the dance floor. We waltzed, sang, and danced the night away.

Kin came from Adelaide, Rockhampton, Woorabinda, to attend the event. Cousins who hadn't seen each other in ages couldn't believe how their families had grown. The Holt name will live on for a long time if the offspring are anything to go by. I felt so proud of my family as they were all there, apart from my lost loved ones.

That weekend we had seventeen people living in our house (it is not unusual for some Aboriginals to have more than that all the time) and it was wonderful. It felt like old times again. It reminded me of Inala days when the Bond boys would come down and make themselves at home and bring their girlfriends and friends, and when my friends who were in need of a place to stay the night would camp over. My house was always open and welcome to them.

The weekend was topped off with a barbecue at my brother Albert's place. We gathered in the backyard and told stories about the past and present, joked, laughed and reminisced about the old days. It was so lovely to have us all together.

Sadly, my dear sister Ruby was not with us. She had passed away in September 1990. My then surviving brothers Jimmy, Oliver, Albert and Walter and sisters Thelma and Isobel attended her funeral. Margaret, unfortunately, was in hospital. There are only six of us left now. Ruby was the most popular of all our family. She had a loving personality and got on well with all her brothers and sisters, nieces and nephews and their children as well. Fond of gambling, we sometimes went to the pokies in Tweed for a day's outing. She suffered two strokes and the last one took its toll severely. My darling sister could not speak and never fully recovered. She is sadly missed by all. She is at rest now in a peaceful corner of a Brisbane cemetery.

My children have always said I grieve like no one else they've seen. I do have an intensity of feelings which well up inside me. Reminiscing all the wonderful times I have spent with my loved ones gives me much comfort and I know they are never completely gone as their spirits are always with us.

It is the memories of loved ones, and their children who are with us, that bring so much joy and pleasure. A loved one can never be forgotten because they live within everyone who has known and touched their lives so deeply. This is how it has been with all my passed love ones.

Ruby with her daughter Denise Randall, 1989

Having the Last Say

I HAD BEEN THINKING about the place I began my days as a domestic as a girl. That first place, Barcudgel Station via Charleville, had been on my mind. Something was calling me to it. I wanted to go, but how could I find it now, nearly sixty years later? It would have changed its name so many times it would be hard to trace.

In 1991, we went on a trip to Cunnamulla to visit our friends, Brian and Jenny Shillingsworth and family. There was me and Jackie and John Henry and our friend Bobby Hagen who came from Cunnamulla. I wanted to try to get back to Barcudgel, so from Cunnamulla we travelled north to Charleville. The others didn't hold out much hope, but I was determined. When we got to Charleville, they went to the cafe and I went into the police station to ask directions to Barcudgel. I couldn't believe my luck — the receptionist was the daughter of the people who now owned Barcudgel. She rang her mother straight away to tell her about us and then she wrote down the directions. I came out waving excitedly to Jackie and Bobby, and I'm sure they thought I was womba. They told me that I'd taken so long in the police station that they thought I'd been locked up. You should have seen the look on their faces when I said, 'Let's go! I've got the address'.

155

Bobby navigated and Jackie drove. Go about thirty kilometres down the Quilpie Road, cross two rivers, come to a railway line, pass house on left, turn left at grid, through gate at top of hill, left a broken-down sign, left at fork in road. And there we found a neat country house.

I went round to the back of the house and introduced myself to Mrs Hogden. I came back to the others and said, 'Jack, this isn't Barcudgel Station'. My poor daughter nearly collapsed, gunin gunin.

But we were close. Barcudgel adjoined the Hogden property, and Mrs Hogden would take us over there. But first she warmly welcomed us to a cup of tea and a huge, home-baked cake. How times have changed, I thought. Sixty years ago, it was me waiting on white visitors, making the tea. As she poured the tea she apologised for the tea leaves in my cup and, nodding in the direction of the old homestead, said, 'If you'd been making the tea over there, it would have been you straining the tea'. We all laughed. Truer words were never spoken.

Mrs Hogden took us over to the old bore. I used to cart water every day from here to the house. It still had much life in it. Water was flowing furiously. The moss and lush grass surrounding it made it an oasis in a desert. The place was so dry then. The country was in its worst stage of drought.

We then went to the old place. The others drove the half kilometre but I walked. I wanted the memories to come back to me of the days when I was a young girl in a grown-up's world. When I got to the place, I was saddened by what I saw. The station house had been burnt down by bushfire some years earlier. There were a few things still among the ruins. I found an old mincer that I probably had held in my working hands. The old frame of the shearing sheds still stood. I looked around me at these ruins and tears welled up in my eyes. I had come back as a grown woman to that early place that had such hard memories, and I thought of the many good years that had passed since.

I saw my life pass before me on that day, at that special place. The memories and the tears came flooding back. I had mixed feelings. I thought about how the white people treated us and how they misunderstood us and still do today. I thought about how they could never keep us down. But more, I thought about being given the privilege of being born Aboriginal.

When I think of my life now, although the lives of Aboriginal people have always been hard, I wouldn't change being Aboriginal for the world — except, as Ernie Dingo says, at four o'clock in the morning trying to hail a taxi in Brisbane.

Glossaries

Aboriginal language words from Wakka Wakka and Pitjara

barjan poison

binagurrie skinny legs

binungunj deaf

bogey bath

bookah nasal congestion

brunjabai pregnant

bungu money

bunthie bottom

cooliman artefact for carrying babies, water, food

dorry stickybeak

gamon only joking, pretending

gooly up wild

gudja smelly

guvung egg

guna pooh

gunduburrie baby, small child

gunin gunin poor thing

GLOSSARIES

gunyah house

jinung foot

mardie Aboriginal person

migaloos white people

muntha bread

munyarl/myall shy person

munyoos lice

ngumuns breasts

niggi niggi making love

Nunga South Australian Aboriginal person

thilly-wujaburri big white eyes watching me

thimbun female

withew white person

womba mad

woomera artefact for throwing spears

yarraman horse

yuki oh no

yunjilbai larrikin

Aboriginal English

deadliest magical

d-o-n-t don't be like that

good-go tell me another one

jarred stumped

knock off stop it

savvy understand

which way how come

werd word